Cambridge Elements ≡

Elements in Environmental, Natural Resource
and Sustainable Development Economics
edited by
Phoebe Koundouri
*Athens University of Economics and Business
(Greece) & University of Cambridge (UK)*

AF234798

ENVIRONMENTAL ECONOMICS IN THE PRESENCE OF TIPPING POINTS

Aart de Zeeuw
Tilburg University

CAMBRIDGE
UNIVERSITY PRESS

CAMBRIDGE
UNIVERSITY PRESS

Shaftesbury Road, Cambridge CB2 8EA, United Kingdom

One Liberty Plaza, 20th Floor, New York, NY 10006, USA

477 Williamstown Road, Port Melbourne, VIC 3207, Australia

314–321, 3rd Floor, Plot 3, Splendor Forum, Jasola District Centre,
New Delhi – 110025, India

Cambridge University Press is part of Cambridge University Press & Assessment,
a department of the University of Cambridge.

We share the University's mission to contribute to society through the pursuit of
education, learning and research at the highest international levels of excellence.

www.cambridge.org
Information on this title: www.cambridge.org/9781009688703

DOI: 10.1017/9781009688673

First published 2026

A catalogue record for this publication is available from the British Library

*A Cataloging-in-Publication data record for this Element is available
from the Library of Congress*

ISBN 978-1-009-68870-3 Hardback
ISBN 978-1-009-68871-0 Paperback
ISSN 2977-747X (online)
ISSN 2977-7461 (print)

Cambridge University Press & Assessment has no responsibility for the persistence
or accuracy of URLs for external or third-party internet websites referred to in this
publication and does not guarantee that any content on such websites is, or will remain,
accurate or appropriate.

For EU product safety concerns, contact us at Calle de José Abascal, 56, 1°, 28003
Madrid, Spain, or email eugpsr@cambridge.org

Environmental Economics in the Presence of Tipping Points

Elements in Environmental, Natural Resource and Sustainable Development Economics

DOI: 10.1017/9781009688673
First published online: April 2026

Aart de Zeeuw
Tilburg University

Author for correspondence: Aart de Zeeuw,
A.J.deZeeuw@tilburguniversity.edu

Abstract: Environmental economics is growing rapidly. It is simply not sufficient to consider consumption, production, and welfare in isolation from the natural environment. Integrating ecological systems in economic analysis requires the possible occurrence of tipping points or regime shifts to be taken into account. This Element focuses on two recent developments in environmental economics theory. One is economic management of ecological systems with tipping points, with the lake as the classical example. The other one is investigating the consequences of uncertain possible shocks to parameters in economic models, with the carrying capacity in a fishery and total factor productivity (due to climate tipping) in Ramsey growth as examples. This Element provides a precise account of the concepts, techniques, and results in the analysis of these models, which shows the effects of tipping and allows for other applications. It starts with a broader list of examples and management options.

Keywords: tipping points, pollution control, international agreements, fishery, Ramsey growth

ISBNs: 9781009688703 (HB), 9781009688710 (PB), 9781009688673 (OC)
ISSNs: 2977-747X (online), 2977-7461 (print)

Contents

1 Introduction

Environmental economics is a branch of economics that is becoming increasingly important. It is simply not sufficient to consider consumption, production, and welfare in isolation from the natural environment. The constant interaction between economic systems and the natural environment (in the sense of pollution and extracting resources) implies that the natural capital changes. This may not be so important when the natural capital is abundant and the shadow price of changes is small, but economic activities have increased up to a level that changes in the natural environment cannot be ignored anymore. Nature has many values in terms of life support and the provision of all sorts of ecosystem services. The Club of Rome put out a warning that this may get lost with a focus on the availability of resources (Meadows et al., 1972), but economists were not immediately alarmed because they trusted the mechanism of scarcity, higher prices, and the search for alternatives. This changed when the concern shifted from the availability of certain resources to the protection of the ecosystems that provide a wide variety of resources and services. A good example is the shift from concern about the availability of fossil fuels to concern about the accumulation of CO_2 and climate change by burning these fossil fuels (Stern, 2007). The mindset of economics is changing. Instead of analyzing consumption, production, and welfare in isolation, economic analysis must integrate the interactions with the natural environment and consider the consequences for the provision of ecosystem services in consumption, production, and welfare.

Integrating ecological systems, or ecosystems, into economic analysis implies that characteristics of ecosystems must be considered. An important characteristic is the occurrence of *tipping points* or *regime shifts*. A regime shift is a large, abrupt, and persistent change in structure and functioning of an ecosystem (Biggs et al., 2012). The shift happens suddenly at a tipping point. The ecosystem remains in the other regime for a long time, and may or may not tip back to the original regime. The seminal paper was on an insect outbreak and the interaction of the insects with predators and the foliage of trees (Ludwig et al., 1978). The foliage is both food and protection from predators. Abundance of foliage leads to an insect outbreak. At some point, the foliage (food) is gone, which also attracts predators, and then the insect density jumps back to a low number. These patterns occur everywhere in nature (Scheffer et al., 2001). It becomes relevant for economics when human activities are involved, and valuable ecosystem services are lost in a regime shift. A good example is a lake (Scheffer, 1998; Carpenter, 2003). At some point, an increase in the release of phosphorus from agriculture into the lake tips the lake from blue water to green soup. Ecosystem services such as clean water, fish, and recreation are lost. A significant decrease in the release of phosphorus is needed to tip the lake back to its pristine state, and in some situations, the regime shift is irreversible. In any case, a trade-off occurs between agricultural benefits and a possible sudden loss of ecosystem services that is difficult or impossible to restore. Economics in the presence of tipping points is born.

The issue of stability gives another perspective on regime shifts and tipping points. A regime is a domain of attraction in the sense that for a given input, the ecosystem returns to the equilibrium in the case of a disturbance within that domain. However, in the case of a larger disturbance, the stability is lost, and the ecosystem converges to a different equilibrium, with other properties. Furthermore, for an increasing input, the equilibrium remains in the same regime up to a point, but at that point, a small increase in input causes the ecosystem to shift to another regime, so that the stability is lost. The ecosystem converges to an equilibrium in the other regime, with other properties. From a mathematical perspective, the equilibria of such an ecosystem (as a function of the input) have a concave–convex shape, such that for a certain range of inputs, the ecosystem has three equilibria: two stable and one unstable. Stability of the good equilibrium is lost if the disturbance is too large. Furthermore, increasing the input just above this range also implies that the good equilibrium is lost, so that the ecosystem shifts to the other regime. A good example is the lake system. Extensive studying and testing have shown that this type of modelling captures data and behavior of lakes quite well. The lake model is the basis for the economic analysis in Section 3.

The economics profession responded in two ways to the possible occurrence of tipping points in natural systems. First, the standard economic analysis of the trade-off between the benefits of the polluting activities and the loss of ecosystem services is extended in the case where a model for the ecosystem exists and is subject to a possible regime shift. Because such a model is a dynamical model, optimal management is an optimal control problem with a concave–convex constraint. This technique was introduced in economics a long time ago for an optimal growth model with a concave–convex production function (Skiba, 1978). This paper did not draw much attention because such a production function was not considered realistic, but the technique revived because such a curve is very realistic for the equilibria of an ecosystem with a tipping point. Furthermore, an ecosystem is often common property, with several users. This implies that the optimal control problem turns into a differential game. Section 3 shows the optimal control solution (Brock and Starrett, 2003) and differential game equilibria (Mäler et al., 2003) for the lake system. Lack of cooperation may imply that the lake ends up in a saddle-point stable steady state in the regime with a low level of ecosystem services, whereas it is best to end up in the regime with a high level. By levying a tax on pollution, a regulator can try to achieve the optimal management outcome. In the absence of a regulator, a stable coalition of users is needed to prevent tipping to the bad regime.

Second, standard economic models with a parameter that represents the natural environment are extended with a hazard rate. This hazard rate gives the probability of a shock to the parameter at some point in time, and this represents the potential tipping point. An example is the fishery model, where tipping in the ecosystem causes a shock to the carrying capacity of the fishery (Polasky et al., 2011). Another example is the Ramsey growth model, where climate tipping causes a shock to the total factor productivity (van der Ploeg and de Zeeuw, 2019). A hazard rate affects the outcome of the economic analysis, especially if the hazard rate is endogenous and depends on the choices that are made. For example, a low stock of fish increases the hazard rate of tipping in the ecosystem, and a high stock of greenhouse gases increases the hazard rate of climate tipping. Section 4 shows the effect of a potential tipping point on the standard results in these models. Hazard rates are not new in economic analysis (Kamien and Schwartz, 1971; Cropper, 1976) but they usually apply to a possible collapse in stock or utility. However, a tipping point in an ecological system means a change in the system dynamics rather than such a collapse. A total collapse implies that the hazard rate acts as a discount rate. Note that a partial collapse of the stock does not change the dynamics and the resulting equilibrium. A change in the system dynamics, however, leads to precautionary behavior and additional tax rates. These differences become clear in Section 4.

Sections 3 and 4 provide a precise analysis of the two main responses of the economics profession to the possible occurrence of tipping points in natural systems. The purpose of these sections is to show the main insights and to provide the techniques to analyze these types of problems. However, the models are specific and do not provide a broader view on tipping points, and do not sufficiently justify the wider range of policy options. Therefore, Section 2 also discusses some other examples of tipping points in ecosystems, with a broader management discussion. The concept of a tipping point is not restricted to ecological systems, it also pops up in the description of socioeconomic behavior. The shift from smoking to nonsmoking in society is a good example. Herd behavior in investment (Scharfstein and Stein, 1990) and in the spreading of ideas (Bikhchandani et al., 1992; Gladwell, 2000) is also related to the concept of a tipping point. This Element focuses on tipping points originating in ecological systems, and the effect of this on economic models and economic analysis. Extensions to socioeconomic tipping points is left for further research.

2 Managing Ecosystems with Tipping Points

A simple example of a tipping point occurred in Australia (Walker et al., 2010). Groundwater has little or no impact on agricultural productivity until the water table reaches about two meters below the surface. At this point, capillary action draws water to the surface, leading to salinization of the topsoil and dramatically reducing crop growth. Rainfall is exogenous and uncertain, so that input is not under control, but management can install pumps or restore the native vegetation to keep the water table low. Choosing a larger margin of safety below the two meters reduces the risk that the water table will rise to the critical level but increases the costs. Managing the ecosystem requires balancing the costs with the reduced risk. This risk depends on the expected pattern of rainfall and on the damage to agriculture for the time the water table is above the critical level.

2.1 The Lake

The most famous example is the lake system, which is the basis for the analysis in Section 3. In a clear lake, rooted plants absorb the excess phosphorus in the water, which prevents algae blooms. However, when phosphorus levels exceed the absorptive capacity of the rooted plants, the excess nutrients cause algae to grow and to reduce the light penetration, which leads to the death of rooted plants. This in turn destabilizes the phosphorus trapped in the sediment of the lake, which further fuels algae growth (Carpenter, 2003). The lake shifts from a so-called oligotrophic regime to a so-called eutrophic regime, with a loss of ecosystem services, such as clean water, fish, and recreation. Oligotrophic and eutrophic are trophic (or nutritional) classifications of a lake that indicate the biological productivity of a lake and the availability of nutrients such as phosphorus. Oligotrophic means a low level of biological productivity and therefore a good water quality. Eutrophic means a high level of biological productivity and therefore a poor water quality. It takes a long time and a large reduction in phosphorus levels before the lake shifts back to the oligotrophic regime. The return to the good regime may even be impossible. When the input of phosphorus originates from agriculture, managing the lake requires balancing agricultural benefits of using the lake as a waste sink with the loss of ecosystem services. Limnologists have extensively studied the lake system. There are also studies comparing costs and benefits of eutrophication control measures in specific lakes (Hein, 2006). Section 3 derives the structure for the analysis of the trade-off in various situations: optimal management, common property, and including fast and slow variables.

2.2 The Coral Reef

Another famous example is the bleaching of a coral-reef system. A small increase in the maximum temperature of the ocean shifts the coral reef from a coral-dominated regime to an algae-dominated regime. Other factors that cause this shift are overfishing of certain species, which affects the food web, and the run-off of nutrients from the agriculture on land (Nyström et al., 2000; Hughes et al., 2003). The bleaching and the ultimate loss of coral reefs causes damage to fisheries, tourism, and shoreline protection. Management is difficult because the causes of the regime shift are partly local (agriculture on land), partly regional (overfishing), and partly global (climate change). The damage is mainly local but only local management fails because it cannot control climate change and overfishing by outside fishing companies. Overfishing also hurts the fishing companies, because the ecosystem shifts and the fish disappear, but the fishing companies operating globally move elsewhere. However, at some point, there are no places to move to anymore (Berkes et al., 2006).

2.3 Engineering

The last two examples could possibly be manipulated by releasing certain fish species in the lake or around the coral reef. This affects the food web and may keep algae blooms down. However, this engineering of nature must be carefully studied to prevent unwanted side effects (Crutzen, 2006). In the case of a coral reef, it means replacing the species that is overfished by a species that can play the same role in the ecosystem. In general, a good management principle is to keep diversity and redundancy of species in an ecosystem (Elmquist et al., 2003). When, for example, a virus hits one of the species, another species can take over (Norberg et al., 2001). High species diversity within the functional group of herbivores on coral reefs increases the probability that the grazing function on algae stays intact during shocks such as a virus outbreak. Management takes a risk when it only focuses on immediate economic benefits but increases the vulnerability of the ecosystem. For example, the lobster fishery in Maine was very successful in the sense that lobsters were abundant, because management succeeded to turn them into the dominant species, but if the lobsters were hit, the ecosystem would collapse too (Steneck et al., 2011). It is also a good management principle to keep diversity in the economic activities. For example, when the cod in West Greenland disappeared, the villages that had specialized in cod almost disappeared, but the villages that had diversified into cod and shrimp could easily shift and grow (Hamilton et al., 2000).

2.4 Uncertainty

A major issue in managing ecosystems with tipping points is the uncertainty, both about the precise location of the threshold and about the precise effects when the threshold is crossed. In a case where tipping has occurred in the same type of ecosystem, this knowledge can be used to model the ecosystem and estimate the parameters. The lake system is a good example. Moreover, adaptive management in the form of active experimentation is a strategy that accepts costs by experimenting with some lakes to learn about these ecosystems, and uses this knowledge to prevent tipping and subsequent costs for other lakes now and in the future. However, experimentation is not always possible or advisable when a system is unique and has substantial value. For example, it is expected that the climate may have tipping points, but experimentation may trigger harmful regime shifts, which is the outcome that experimentation is designed to learn about and avoid. At the global scale, possible climate tipping is one of the nine so-called planetary boundaries (Rockström et al., 2009). Two other examples are boundaries for biodiversity and for phosphorus and nitrogen cycles. A recent paper shows that six of the nine planetary boundaries have already been crossed, including the three mentioned earlier (Richardson et al., 2023). It is expected that crossing the boundaries will cause huge damage. Planetary boundaries have a range of uncertainty, but it is hard to get precise information on the threshold and the costs of crossing it. The argument of the paper on the planetary boundaries is to stay on the safe side and to keep, for example, global warming below a certain limit.

If the location of the threshold is uncertain but it is not possible to experiment, it is important to find ways to detect whether the threshold is close or not. A problem with tipping points is that it is difficult to see them coming because the conditions of the ecosystem before tipping stay basically the same and then suddenly change when the system tips. However, by taking a closer look at the dynamics of the ecosystem, it is possible to detect when the stability is weakening. For example, an increased autocorrelation or an increased variance are early-warning signals that the system is approaching a tipping point (Brock and Carpenter, 2006; Scheffer et al., 2009). The case of the lake distinguishes three timescales: The loading of phosphorus is slow, the stock of phosphorus in the water of the lake adjusts rather quickly, and the random disturbances are fast. Before the loading of phosphorus changes, the stock of phosphorus reaches an equilibrium, and if this equilibrium is close to a tipping point, the variance of the random disturbances increases. This indicator does not require detailed knowledge of the system dynamics.

2.5 Management under Uncertainty

In general, optimal management faces a combination of uncertainty and the complexity of possible tipping points in an ecosystem. An example is managing a rangeland that is subject to uncertain rainfall patterns and can shift from a grass-dominated regime to a shrub-dominated regime. A full stochastic optimal control analysis combining these two aspects is complicated, but it is possible to develop so-called robust management strategies and to show that responding to rainfall variability increases the returns considerably (Janssen et al., 2004). Optimal management of the lake model introduced in Section 2.1 can also be extended with uncertainty, which leads to a stochastic optimal control problem that has been solved (see Section 3.2).

Uncertainty also means that even if management aims to avoid the threshold, tipping can occur, and it is important to be prepared. Resources must be divided between investments in efforts to prevent tipping (mitigation) and investments in capabilities to face the consequences when tipping occurs (adaptation). The right mix and size of these investments depends on the probability of a shift, the degree of reversibility of the shift, the extent to which well-being is affected by the shift, and the relative cost of mitigation and adaptation investments.

If more information about the location of the threshold and/or the effect of crossing the threshold is expected in the future, this is a reason to be more careful, wait for the information, and determine the policy later. In this case, there is a value of waiting like the quasi-option value in the choice to develop or preserve, which arises because of the irreversibility of development (Arrow and Fisher, 1974). Crossing the threshold is a similar issue since it is irreversible or costly to reverse.

Another angle to management under uncertainty is focusing on a standard economic model, such as the fishery or the Ramsey growth model, where the uncertainty is a possible shift of a parameter because of tipping in the ecological system. This angle extends economic theory and is one of the main topics of this Element (see the Introduction and Section 4).

2.6 Concluding Remarks

This section provided a few examples of ecological systems with tipping points and discussed some management issues. It is based on Crépin et al. (2012), which contains many more examples. The website www.regimeshifts .org has an extensive list of ecological systems with tipping points. The literature grew fast in the last decades. Folke et al. (2004) provides a nice introduction.

3 Managing the Lake

Section 2.1 briefly describes the mechanism in the lake that causes the possible regime shift. This section introduces a model that limnologists developed to simulate the behavior of the lake. The core of the model is an equation for the accumulation of phosphorus in the water of the lake. This equation contains a term that can explain tipping behavior and is used in many other models. The term is called a type-III S-shaped functional response (Holling, 1959), and it is responsible for the concave–convex shape of the equilibria of the lake. The second equation describes the phosphorus cycle in the sediment of the lake. The dynamics of this equation is very slow, and initially, this state variable is assumed to be constant so that it becomes a parameter of the first equation. Section 3.5 provides an analysis of the lake with the combined fast–slow dynamics. Finally, the third equation describes the loading of phosphorus on the lake, but this describes past human behavior and must be replaced in optimal economic analysis, by turning loading into a control variable.

3.1 The Lake Model

The lake model, with loading of phosphorus L as a control variable, is given by (Carpenter, 2005)

$$
\begin{aligned}
\dot{P}(t) &= L(t) - (w_1 + w_2)P(t) + rM(t)\frac{P^d(t)}{P^d(t) + m^d}, P(0) = P_0, \\
\dot{M}(t) &= w_1 P(t) - w_3 M(t) - rM(t)\frac{P^d(t)}{P^d(t) + m^d}, M(0) = M_0,
\end{aligned}
\tag{1}
$$

where P denotes the phosphorus density in the lake water, and M in the lake sediment (with M for mud). The parameter w_1 denotes the sedimentation rate, w_2 the outflow rate, w_3 the permanent burial rate, t is time, and r the maximum recycling rate. The parameter values in the lake model (1), with the nonlinear type-III functional response term, are estimated and tested using observations on Lake Mendota in Wisconsin: $w_1 = 0.7$, $w_2 = 0.15$, $w_3 = 0.001$, $r = 0.019$, $m = 2.4$, $d = 8$. The small values of r and w_3 imply that the dynamics of the second equation (Equation 1) is much slower than the dynamics of the first equation (Janssen and Carpenter, 1999). The analysis first assumes that M is constant. Section 3.5 returns to the full model (Equation 1) and provides the analysis with the fast and slow dynamics in P and M.

Assuming M is constant, so that Equation 1 reduces to a differential equation in P, rewriting $x = P/m$, $a = L/rM$, $b = (w_1 + w_2)m/rM$, changing the power to $d = 2$ (to simplify without affecting the qualitative structure of the results), and changing the time scale to rMt/m yields

$$\dot{x}(t) = a(t) - bx(t) + \frac{x^2(t)}{x^2(t) + 1}, x(0) = x_0. \tag{2}$$

Equation 2 represents the essential dynamics of a lake (Carpenter et al., 1999), and it has been used in a series of papers, starting with Brock and Starrett (2003), Mäler et al. (2003), and Wagener (2003). Equation 2 has also been used as representing, in general, pollution of an ecosystem in an environmental economic analysis (e.g., Heijdra and Heijnen, 2013). The state variable x represents the phosphorus density in the lake water, the control variable a represents the loading of phosphorus on the lake, and b is the only remaining parameter. Research on lakes all over the world has shown that this parameter can vary over a wide range.

The steady states or equilibria of the lake model (Equation 2) are given by

$$a = bx - \frac{x^2}{x^2 + 1}, \tag{3}$$

and are represented by the concave–convex curve in Figure 1.

Figure 1 shows the two types of instabilities discussed in the Introduction. For the loading $\bar{a}$, the lake has two stable equilibria, that is, x_1 in the oligotrophic regime of the lake, with a high level of ecosystem services, and x_3 in the eutrophic regime of the lake, with a low level of ecosystem services. If the disturbance from the equilibrium x_1 is too large and beyond the level of the unstable equilibrium x_2, the regime shifts, and the lake converges to the equilibrium x_3. Moreover, if the loading $\bar{a}$ is increased, the equilibria in the oligotrophic regime reach the tipping point where a small increase in loading shifts the lake to the eutrophic regime. Then it takes a big reduction in loading to shift the lake back to the oligotrophic regime (a hysteresis effect). Note that tipping occurs when the stable equilibrium x_1 or x_3 coincides with the unstable one x_2. In mathematics, this is called a bifurcation or catastrophe (Zeeman, 1976; Rinaldi and Scheffer, 2000). Note also that the structure with the two stable equilibria and one unstable equilibrium disappears when the curve in Figure 1 is stretched out and loses the local maximum and the local minimum where the tipping occurs. Furthermore, when the right part of the curve in Figure 1 is pulled down, so that the local minimum moves below the axis, tipping becomes irreversible: Tipping back is not possible because the loading cannot be negative. The situation that occurs depends on the value of the parameter b. If $b \geq 3\sqrt{3}/8$, there is one equilibrium for each level of loading. If $b \leq 0.5$, tipping is irreversible. If $0.5 < b < 3\sqrt{3}/8$, Figure 1 applies, with two tipping points and hysteresis. The last situation is the most interesting one and forms the basis for the following economic analysis.

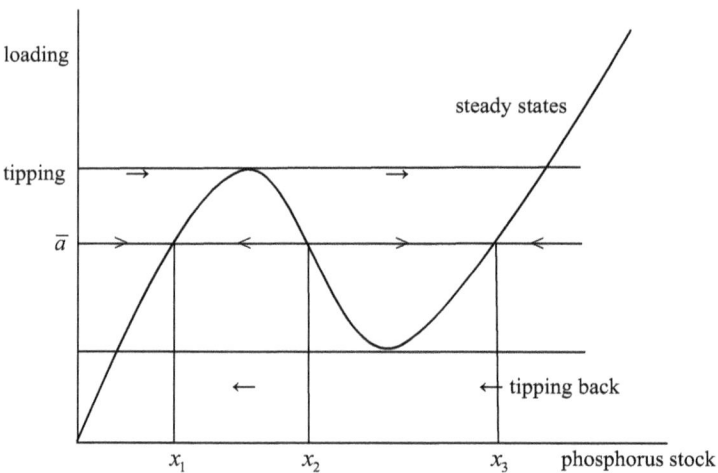

Figure 1 Lake model.

3.2 Optimal Management

The agricultural benefits, as a function of the loading a, of using the lake as a waste sink must be balanced with the loss of ecosystem services, as a function of the stock x. The objective of optimal management is to find the path of loadings $a(.)$ that maximizes the intertemporal discounted net benefits. The problem becomes

$$\max_{a(.)} \int_0^\infty e^{-\rho t}[\ln a(t) - \gamma x^2(t)]dt, \tag{4}$$

subject to Equation 2, where ρ denotes the discount rate.

It is convenient to take a logarithmic benefit function (Section 3.3) and a quadratic cost function. The parameter γ indicates the relative weight.

Using Pontryagin's maximum principle, the current-value Hamiltonian function becomes

$$H(x, a, \lambda) = \ln a - \gamma x^2 + \lambda\left(a - bx + \frac{x^2}{x^2+1}\right), \tag{5}$$

where λ denotes the co-state, also called the shadow value, and the necessary conditions become the differential Equation 2 and

$$\lambda = -\frac{1}{a}, \dot{\lambda}(t) = \left(\rho + b - \frac{2x(t)}{\left(x^2(t)+1\right)^2}\right)\lambda(t) + 2\gamma x(t), \tag{6}$$

or

$$\dot{a}(t) = -\left(\rho + b - \frac{2x(t)}{\left(x^2(t) + 1\right)^2}\right) a(t) + 2\gamma x(t) a^2(t). \tag{7}$$

The steady states of Equation 7 are given by

$$a = \frac{\rho + b}{2\gamma x} - \frac{1}{\gamma(x^2 + 1)^2}. \tag{8}$$

The left panel of Figure 2 shows the phase diagram for $b = 0.6$, $\rho = 0.03$, and $\gamma = 1$, with the curves reflecting the steady-state equations (Equations 3 and 8). For this value of b, the curve for the steady states of the lake is stretched out when compared to Figure 1, but it still has two tipping points. For these values of ρ and γ, there is one saddle-point stable steady state for the dynamical system (Equations 2 and 7) in the oligotrophic regime of the lake. Using the transversality conditions, the optimal management path follows the stable manifold, shown in the right panel of Figure 2, and converges to this steady state from each initial condition $x(0) = x_0$. It is always best to clean up the lake.

The solution changes if the parameter γ, which reflects the relative weight of the loss of ecosystem services in relation to the agricultural benefits, decreases to $\gamma = 0.5$. The same thing happens if the discount rate ρ is increased. The left panel of Figure 3 shows the phase diagram. It has two saddle-point stable steady states and one unstable steady state in between (Brock and Starrett, 2003). The right panel of Figure 3 shows the solution trajectories of the dynamical system

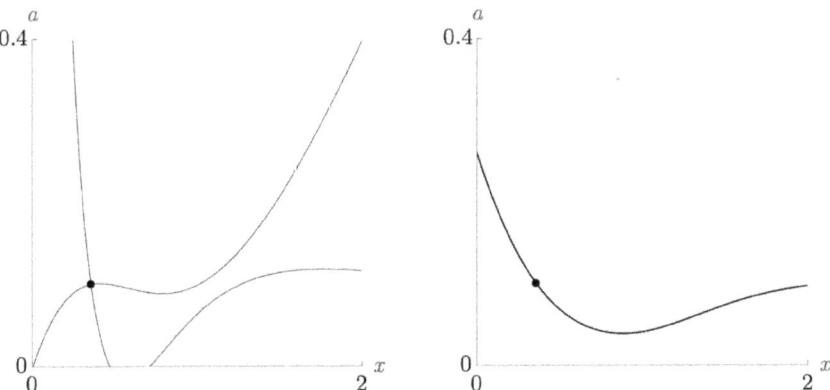

Figure 2 Optimal management, cost parameter 1.

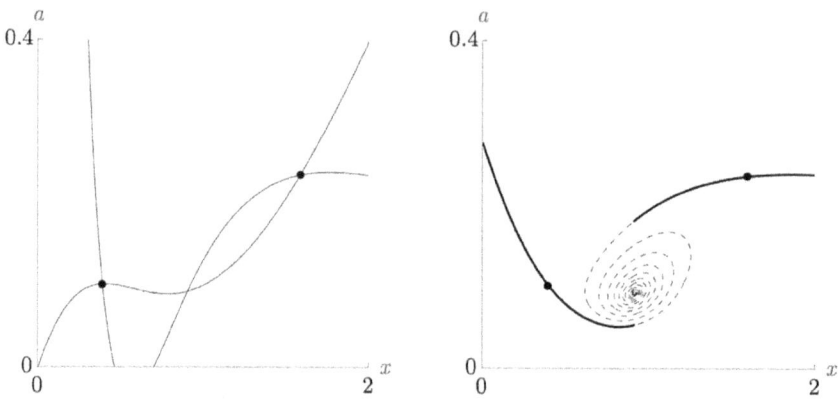

Figure 3 Optimal management, cost parameter 0.5, Skiba point.

(Equations 2 and 7) that curl out of the unstable steady state and either converge to the steady state in the oligotrophic regime or to the steady state in the eutrophic regime. These are candidates for the optimal trajectory. If the initial condition x_0 is situated below the curls, it is clearly better to jump to the lower curve or to the upper curve instead of to some path inside the curls. Whether it is better to jump to the lower curve and converge to the oligotrophic regime or to the upper curve and converge to the eutrophic regime depends on the value of the objective (Equation 4). It is possible to prove that an initial condition $\bar{x}_0$ exists such that these values are the same (Mäler et al., 2003). This is the so-called Skiba point or indifference point. It means that for initial conditions $x_0 \leq \bar{x}_0$, the optimal management path moves to the oligotrophic steady state, and for initial conditions $x_0 \geq \bar{x}_0$ to the eutrophic steady state. It follows that if the relative weight of the loss of ecosystem services γ is small, and if the lake is already very polluted, it is best to accept the costs and to enjoy the higher benefits. However, if the lake is not so polluted yet, it is best to clean it up.

The right panel of Figure 3 resembles the dynamics found in a model for external economies with multiple steady states (Krugman, 1991). That paper argues that for initial conditions outside the curls, the economy moves to the left or to the right but if the history has led to a state below the curls, expectations are needed to determine where the economy ends up. However, in the model in this section, the objective determines the outcome so that only history matters, and not expectations.

The analysis changes when uncertainty is added to the lake model (Dechert and O'Donnell, 2006). For the lake model given by Equation 2, the literature has focused on the situation where Gaussian white noise with a certain intensity is added to the parameter b representing the rate of loss (Grass et al., 2015;

Koutsimpela and Loulakis, 2024). The analysis is complicated, but the main result is quite intuitive. Suppose that the optimal management outcome for the deterministic version of the lake model is depicted in Figure 3. For small values of the noise intensity, the optimal management of the stochastic version also has two attractors, but these are stochastic, and the noise eventually induces a fluctuation that drives the lake into the basin of attraction of the other stochastic attractor. This leads to a pattern where the lake fluctuates for some time around the attractor in one regime and then switches to fluctuate for some time around the attractor in the other regime, and so on. By increasing the intensity of the noise, the picture changes and bifurcations occur. Details of the analysis are beyond the scope of this Element.

3.3 Common Property

An ecosystem is usually common property and therefore vulnerable to a tragedy of the commons (Hardin, 1968). In the case of more users of the ecosystem, each one may argue that more pollution yields more benefits but hardly changes the ecosystem. The problem is that if all the users argue in this way, the ecosystem may be finally destroyed. However, this process stops when the marginal benefit of the individual polluter is equal to its marginal cost. This may not lead to full destruction, but it is interesting to derive the outcome and to compare it with optimal management (Dasgupta, 1982). This turns the issue into the difference between cooperation and noncooperation. The equilibrium in which each polluter behaves optimally in reaction to the other polluters is the Nash equilibrium. This problem is a game, and the game in which the individual optimization problems are dynamical optimal control problems is called a differential game.

Differential games have different Nash equilibria, depending on the commitment level and on the information the polluters have on the pollution stock (Başar and Olsder, 1982). Using Pontryagin's maximum principle, with strategies that only depend on time, leads to what is called the open loop Nash equilibrium. Since the polluters do not get new information on the stock, they do not change their strategies, so that they are effectively committed to their strategies. However, using dynamic programming means that the strategies depend on time and on the stock of pollution. The polluters acquire information on the stock of pollution and wait with choosing their action until they get this information, so that they are not committed. Using dynamic programming leads to what is called the feedback Nash or Markov perfect equilibrium (Section 3.4). An important issue is whether a tax on pollution can induce the polluters to choose optimal management strategies.

Suppose there are n polluters, loading $a_i, i = 1, 2, \ldots, n$, phosphorus on the lake and having the same net benefits $\ln a_i - \gamma x^2$. When the polluters cooperate, as a benchmark, they maximize the sum of their objective functionals, and the problem becomes

$$\max_{a_1(.),\ldots,a_n(.)} \int_0^\infty e^{-\rho t} \left[\sum_{i=1}^n \ln a_i(t) - n\gamma x^2(t) \right] dt, \tag{9}$$

subject to

$$\dot{x}(t) = \sum_{i=1}^n a_i(t) - bx(t) + \frac{x^2(t)}{x^2(t)+1}, x(0) = x_0. \tag{10}$$

Using Pontryagin's maximum principle, the current-value Hamiltonian function tion becomes

$$H(x, a_1, \ldots, a_n, \lambda) = \sum_{i=1}^n \ln a_i - n\gamma x^2 + \lambda \left(\sum_{i=1}^n a_i - bx + \frac{x^2}{x^2+1} \right), \tag{11}$$

where λ denotes the co-state or shadow value, and the necessary conditions become (10) and

$$\lambda = -\frac{1}{a_i}, i = 1, 2 \ldots, n, \dot{\lambda}(t) = \left(\rho + b - \frac{2x(t)}{\left(x^2(t)+1\right)^2} \right) \lambda(t) + 2n\gamma x(t), \tag{12}$$

or

$$\dot{a}_i(t) = -\left(\rho + b - \frac{2x(t)}{\left(x^2(t)+1\right)^2} \right) a_i(t) + 2n\gamma x(t) a_i^2(t), i = 1, 2, \ldots, n, \tag{13}$$

so that

$$\dot{a}(t) = -\left(\rho + b - \frac{2x(t)}{\left(x^2(t)+1\right)^2} \right) a(t) + 2\gamma x(t) a^2(t), a = \sum_{i=1}^n a_i. \tag{14}$$

The dynamical system consisting of the differential Equations 10 and 14, with a representing the total loading, is the same as the dynamical system consisting of the differential Equations 2 and 7. Note that the cooperative outcome, or the outcome under optimal management, turns out to be independent of the number of polluters n, which follows from taking the logarithmic benefit function in the objective (Equation 4).

The (symmetric) open-loop Nash equilibrium requires to simultaneously solve the problems

$$\max_{a_i(.)} \int_0^\infty e^{-\rho t}[\ln a_i(t) - \gamma x^2(t)]dt, i = 1, 2, \ldots, n, \text{ subject to (10).} \tag{15}$$

Using Pontryagin's maximum principle, the current-value Hamiltonian functions become

$$H_i(x, a_i, \lambda_i) = \ln a_i - \gamma x^2 + \lambda_i \left(a_i + \sum_{j \neq i}^n a_j - bx + \frac{x^2}{x^2 + 1} \right), i = 1, 2, \ldots, n, \tag{16}$$

where λ_i denote the co-states or shadow values, and the necessary conditions become Equation 10 and

$$\lambda_i = -\frac{1}{a_i}, \dot{\lambda}_i(t) = \left(\rho + b - \frac{2x(t)}{\left(x^2(t) + 1\right)^2} \right) \lambda_i(t) + 2\gamma x(t), i = 1, 2, \ldots, n, \tag{17}$$

or

$$\dot{a}_i(t) = -\left(\rho + b - \frac{2x(t)}{\left(x^2(t) + 1\right)^2} \right) a_i(t) + 2\gamma x(t)a_i^2(t), i = 1, 2, \ldots, n, \tag{18}$$

so that

$$\dot{a}(t) = -\left(\rho + b - \frac{2x(t)}{\left(x^2(t) + 1\right)^2} \right) a(t) + 2\frac{\gamma}{n}x(t)a^2(t), a = \sum_{i=1}^n a_i. \tag{19}$$

The dynamical system consisting of the differential Equations 10 and 19 is almost the same as the dynamical system consisting of the differential Equations 10 and 14. The only difference is that the parameter γ becomes γ/n.

This game is an example of a potential game where the Nash equilibrium can be found by maximizing an adapted objective (Monderer and Shapley, 1996). The candidate trajectories for the open-loop Nash equilibrium follow from the analysis in Section 3.2. The parameter γ is a bifurcation parameter (Wagener, 2003), because lowering γ from 1 to 0.5 implies that the dynamical system shifts from having one saddle-point stable steady state to having three steady states, two saddle-point stable and one unstable (Section 3.2). Increasing the number of polluters n from 1 to 2 has the same effect as lowering the parameter γ from 1 to 0.5, where γ is the weight for the loss of ecosystem services in the objective functional.

The conclusion is that for the parameter values $b = 0.6, \rho = 0.03$, and $\gamma = 1$, Figure 2 in Section 3.2 shows the solution for the cooperative outcome. Moreover, if the number of polluters $n = 2$, the combined solid and dashed curves in the right panel of Figure 3 show the candidate trajectories for the open-loop Nash equilibrium, since these are the candidate trajectories for optimal management in case $\gamma = 0.5$. There is not a Skiba point $\bar{x}_0$ as for optimal management, because there is not one objective functional differentiating between the possible trajectories. For initial conditions x_0 below the curls, the open-loop Nash equilibrium is not unique. The trajectories along the upper curve toward the steady state in the eutrophic regime and along the lower curve toward the steady state in the oligotrophic regime are both open-loop Nash equilibria (Grass et al., 2017). In this symmetric game, the values of the objectives are the same for the polluters, so that a separating indifference point can still exist in the sense that the polluters coordinate on the best open-loop Nash equilibrium and move to the oligotrophic or eutrophic steady state depending on the initial condition. However, the value can be everywhere better along the lower curve. In this case, a pollution trap occurs, meaning that if the initial condition lies just to the right of the curls, it is not possible to reach the oligotrophic steady state anymore, and the value jumps down. In such a case, the lack of cooperation is very harmful. If the initial condition is lower, there is also a loss due to the lack of cooperation, but this is not so bad because the lake ends up in the oligotrophic regime, in a steady state close to the optimal management steady state. The numbers for the steady-state stock of phosphorus in this setting are 0.353 for optimal management and 0.393 for the open-loop Nash equilibrium. These numbers are close to the tipping point $x = 0.408$.

If a government can regulate and levy a tax on the loading of phosphorus, it is in principle possible to induce the polluters to choose the trajectory of optimal management. A tax τ on the loading a_i changes the first necessary condition in Equation 17 into $\lambda_i = -1/a_i + \tau$, and this must coincide with the first necessary condition in Equation 12, $\lambda = -1/a_i$. This implies that the tax $\tau = \lambda_i - \lambda$, which covers the difference between the noncooperative and cooperative shadow values λ_i and λ, has the desired result. However, such a tax $\tau(t)$ would have to follow a complicated path over time, and it is not realistic that a government can change the tax continuously. Alternatively, a government can try to implement a trajectory close to optimal management by levying a constant tax that has the desired result in the steady state. For a constant tax τ, Equation 19 becomes

$$\dot{a}(t) = -\left(\rho + b - \frac{2x(t)}{\left(x^2(t) + 1\right)^2}\right)\left(a(t) - \frac{\tau}{n}a^2(t)\right) + 2\frac{\gamma}{n}x(t)a^2(t). \quad (20)$$

If $a*$ is the steady state of optimal management, a constant tax $\tau* = (n-1)/a*$ implies that $a*$ is also the steady state of the open-loop Nash equilibrium, according to Equations 14 and 20. However, the curve of steady states for Equation 20 under the constant tax $\tau*$ differs from the curve of steady states for Equation 14, and the open-loop Nash equilibrium path under the constant tax $\tau*$ differs from the optimal management path. If the number of polluters $n = 2$, the pattern is similar and the paths are close but if the number of polluters $n > 7$, the pattern becomes very complicated and the open-loop Nash equilibrium path under $\tau*$ does not move toward the optimal management steady state when the initial condition x_0 is large (Mäler et al., 2003). For a high number of polluters, the constant tax $\tau*$ does not get the lake out of the eutrophic regime.

3.4 Feedback Nash or Markov Perfect Equilibria

If the polluters can condition their phosphorus loadings on the stock of pollution, and if they can wait with choosing their loadings on observing that stock of pollution, the differential game has a different noncooperative equilibrium called the feedback Nash or Markov perfect equilibrium. It is derived with dynamic programming. In the case of cooperation or optimal management, dynamic programming is just another technique that gives the same result as the maximum principle, but in case of a game, the results differ. In general, the Markov perfect equilibrium is considered more realistic than the open-loop Nash equilibrium (which assumes a long commitment and ignorance about the state of the system), but it is harder to derive. Moreover, even if the differential game is nicely concave, so that the open-loop Nash equilibrium is unique, there is a multiplicity of Markov perfect equilibria (Tsutsui and Mino, 1990; Dockner and Long, 1993). It is interesting, however, that for the lake game, this multiplicity is an advantage because it allows the polluters to coordinate on the best Markov perfect equilibrium that has the steady state close to the optimal management steady state, and the Skiba point or pollution trap disappears (Kossioris et al., 2008).

For optimal management, the dynamic programming or Hamilton–Jacobi–Bellman equation in the current-value function $V(x)$ becomes

$$\rho V(x) = \max_{a}[\ln a - \gamma x^2 + V'(x)(a - f(x))], f(x) = bx - \frac{x^2}{x^2 + 1}. \quad (21)$$

It is easy to see that this gives the same result as the maximum principle if the value function is twice continuously differentiable. By writing $V'(x) = \lambda$, the maximization in Equation 21 is the same as the maximization of the Hamiltonian function (Equation 5). Differentiating Equation 21 with respect to x and taking the maximization condition into account (envelope theorem) gives $\rho V' = -2\gamma x + V''(a - f) - V'f'$. Using $\dot{\lambda} = V''(a - f)$, this yields $\dot{\lambda} = (\rho + f')\lambda + 2\gamma x$, which is the second part of Equation 6.

For a differential game, dynamic programming gives a different Nash equilibrium than the open-loop Nash equilibrium derived with the maximum principle. For the lake game, this feedback Nash or Markov perfect equilibrium follows from the Hamilton–Jacobi–Bellman equations

$$\rho V_i(x) = \max_{a_i} \left[\ln a_i - \gamma x^2 + V_i'(x) \left(a_i + \sum_{j \neq i}^{n} a_j - f(x) \right) \right], i = 1, 2, \ldots, n,$$
$$(22)$$

in the current-value functions $V_i(x), i = 1, \ldots, n$. Because of symmetry, the loadings a_i as well as the value functions $V_i(x)$ are the same for $i = 1, \ldots, n$. The maximization condition is $1/a_i = -V_i'(x)$. The loadings a_i are a function of the stock x. Replacing $V_i'(x)$ by $-1/a_i$, differentiating Equation 22 with respect to x, and replacing $V_i'(x)$ by $-1/a_i$ finally yields a differential equation in $a_i(x)$:

$$[a_i(x) - f(x)]a_i'(x) = -\left(\rho + f'(x)\right)a_i(x) + 2\gamma x a_i^2(x). \quad (23)$$

The left-hand side of Equation 23 clearly shows the connections with optimal management and the open-loop Nash equilibrium. First, if there is only one polluter, the left-hand side can be written as $\dot{a}(t)$ in the time domain, because $\dot{x}(t) = a(t) - f(x(t))$, so that Equation 23 becomes Equation 7 or 14. Second, if there are more polluters, the left-hand side of Equation 23 can be written as $\dot{a}_i(t)$, for the artificial state equation $\dot{x}(t) = a_i(t) - f(x(t))$ in another time domain, and then Equation 23 becomes Equation 18 for the open-loop Nash equilibrium. It follows that either differential Equation 23 must be solved

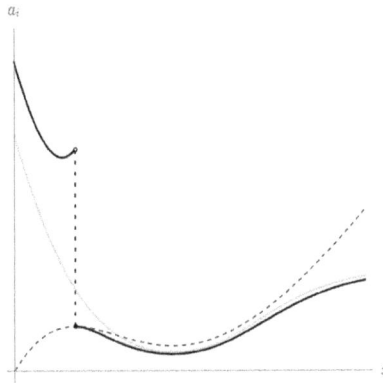

Figure 4 Feedback Nash or Markov perfect equilibria.

(Kossioris et al., 2008) or the artificial system in another time domain must be solved (Dockner and Wagener, 2014). The most important result is that both methods lead to a multiplicity of Markov perfect equilibria. The differential Equation 23 is an Abel differential equation of the second kind (Murphy, 1960). In terms of the individual loading a_i, the steady-state curve for the lake is given by $a_i = f(x)/n$. A way to find the Markov perfect equilibria is to solve the differential equation with boundary conditions $a_i(\hat{x}) = f(\hat{x})/n$, where $\hat{x}$ is a steady state of the lake, and to check the trajectories for stability. A multiplicity of trajectories $a_i(x)$ results that cut the steady-state curve of the lake in a point that is stable. The other way to find the Markov perfect equilibria is to solve the dynamical system with the artificial state equation following from the differential Equation 23. The multiplicity results because in the real system, more stable trajectories occur than the one stable manifold of the artificial system.

Figure 4 shows the solution for the parameter values $b = 0.6$, $\rho = 0.03$, and $\gamma = 1$, and for $n = 2$. The gray curve shows the only solution $a_i(x)$ that is continuous, stable, and defined for each x. It is the stable manifold of the artificial system in the other time domain. The black curve shows another solution with a steady state that is closer to the optimal management steady state. The right part of the black curve is tangent to the steady-state curve of the lake and provides the solution for all the initial conditions to the right of this steady state. It is not possible to get closer to the optimal management steady state, but this steady state converges to the optimal management steady state when the discount rate ρ goes to 0. It is called the best Markov perfect equilibrium, and for these parameter values, the number for this steady-state stock of phosphorus is 0.383. Continuing the black curve to the left below the steady-state curve for the lake is unstable and does not provide the Markov perfect equilibrium for initial conditions to the left of the best Markov perfect steady state (Rubio and Casino, 2002). There is a solution that is defined everywhere, but this requires a discontinuity in the trajectory (Jaakkola and Wagener, 2023). It is given by the full black curve in Figure 4. The polluters start with high loadings of phosphorus, and at some point, jump down to the steady-state loadings. It is hard to imagine this behavior in practice, but it is the only way to have a solution that is defined for each x and reaches the best Markov perfect steady state. The most interesting result is that there is no Skiba point or pollution trap. For an initial condition x_0 in the eutrophic regime, the Markov perfect equilibrium gets the lake out of the eutrophic regime. Interactions between the polluters through the observations on the stock of phosphorus allow for equilibria moving the lake to the oligotrophic regime, although this does not mean that the value of the objective is close to the optimal management value (Kossioris et al., 2008).

As for the open-loop Nash equilibrium, if a government can regulate and levy a tax on the loading of phosphorus, it is in principle possible to induce the polluters to choose the trajectory of optimal management. Because the loadings a_i are a function of the stock x, this tax τ must be a function of the stock x as well. Furthermore, this tax must cover the difference between the noncooperative and cooperative marginal values. However, such a tax $\tau(x)$ would become very complicated, and it is not realistic that a government can implement such a tax. It may be possible to implement a simple tax rule, like a linear tax, with the property that the Markov perfect steady state coincides with the optimal management steady state. However, the value of the objective is then lower than the value under optimal management, especially when the initial condition x_0 is not close to the steady state (Kossioris et al., 2011). The situation improves for more complicated tax rules but the combination of this complexity and the remaining gap in welfare does not make this very attractive either. It is better to try to strike an agreement between the polluters (Section 3.7).

3.5 The Full Lake Model

The simple reduced form (Equation 2) for the lake model ignores the slowly changing stock of phosphorus in the sediment or the "mud" of the lake, and the interaction between the stocks of phosphorus P in the water and M in the mud of the lake, as in the dynamical system (Equation 1) (Carpenter, 2005). This also affects the view on tipping in Figure 1. Tipping not only occurs when the phosphorus loading is increased but may also occur because the tipping point is pulled down due to the slowly changing variable M. This explains why the polluters may be taken by surprise when they only focus on the reduced form of the lake model. This section returns to the full lake model (Equation 1), and gives a short description of a numerical extension to the analysis of optimal management and the lake game for the parameters presented in Section 3.1 for Lake Mendota, but with $d = 2$ (Grass et al., 2017). The framework of fast and slow dynamics is also very relevant for the analysis of climate change (Bala et al., 2010). In these models, slow dynamics refers to the climate response that is associated with a change in surface and deep ocean temperature. Other examples that have fast and slow dynamics are coral reefs subject to fishing pressure (Crépin, 2007) and pest control (Crépin et al., 2011). These examples study polar cases, where either the fast system or the slow system is in equilibrium, but they do not study both the time scales simultaneously. The following analysis determines for the lake model the slow manifold in the actual time scale separation together with the actual path of the fast variable. In this way, Skiba manifolds and solution paths result that are policy relevant but are not identified by studying polar cases or approximations of the slow manifold.

The objective of optimal management is now to find the path of loadings $L(.)$ that maximizes the intertemporal discounted net benefits

$$\max_{L(.)} \int_0^\infty e^{-\rho t} [\ln L(t) - \gamma P^2(t)] dt, \tag{24}$$

subject to Equation 1, where ρ denotes the discount rate. To make the results comparable with the results for the analysis of the reduced form, the parameters are $\rho = 0.0425$, because the time scale is not changed, $\gamma = 1/m^2 = 0.1736$ instead of $\gamma = 1$, and the initial condition $M_0 = 179$, so that $b = 0.6$. The main difference with the analysis of the reduced form is that there are two stock variables now, P and M, so that the necessary conditions following from the current-value Hamiltonian function become a four-dimensional dynamical system in the two stock variables, the loading L and the shadow value of the changes in the stock M. In the case of n polluters, the same applies to the cooperative solution and the open-loop Nash equilibrium. The other important aspect is the difference in time scales for the fast and slow dynamics in the stock variables P and M that can be analyzed simultaneously by using the toolbox named OCMat (http://orcos.tuwien.ac.at/research/ocmat_software).

It is beyond the scope of this Element to present the analysis and the results in detail. Only some interesting results are provided here (Grass et al., 2017). First, for $\gamma = 0.1736$ and starting with the initial conditions $M_0 = 179$ and P_0 either in the oligotrophic or eutrophic regime of the lake, the result is basically the same as the result for the reduced form of the lake. The optimal management path converges to the steady state $(P^*, M^*) = (0.77420, 194.19)$, which is close to what was found for the reduced form of the lake. The adjustment in P is fast, followed by slow adjustments in M and thus P, along the isocline $\dot{P} = 0$. Starting with a higher initial condition $M_0 = 240$, however, a different type of Skiba or indifference point occurs. This Skiba point does not separate different domains of attraction with different steady states but separates different optimal paths toward the same steady state. These paths have the same value for the objective. One path moves fast to the oligotrophic regime of the lake and then slowly adjusts to the long-run steady state. The other path moves to the eutrophic regime first, then slowly adjusts M, and finally moves fast to the long-run steady state in the oligotrophic regime. Apparently, optimal management in this case is indifferent between moving to the oligotrophic regime directly or staying in the eutrophic regime for a while and moving there later. This type of Skiba point is called a weak Skiba point. By lowering M_0, a weak Skiba manifold in the (P, M)-plane appears but at some point, the optimal management path always moves directly to the oligotrophic area, as for $M_0 = 179$. The reason is that lowering M_0 implies that the shape of the lake equilibria changes when M_0 passes the lowest point of the weak Skiba manifold (via the parameter b in the reduced form), so that a bifurcation occurs from three steady states to one. Although the two optimal management paths starting in a weak Skiba point have the same value for the objective, the optimal loading paths $L^*(t)$ differ. The one that moves the system to the eutrophic regime first and then back to the oligotrophic regime is less regular and jumps up and down. Because optimal loading is the inverse of the shadow value of the changes in the stock P, the path of the shadow value is also irregular. This implies that in case a tax is needed to implement the optimal loading path, the tax path is irregular, which is a reason to choose the optimal management path that moves the system directly to the oligotrophic regime.

Second, for $\gamma = 0.1736/2 = 0.0868$ the traditional Skiba or indifference points return. There are two steady states now, one in the oligotrophic regime of the lake and one in the eutrophic regime. The result is basically the same as the result for the reduced form of the lake. A Skiba manifold in the (P, M)-plane appears that separates the domains of attraction for the two steady states. Starting with the initial conditions $M_0 = 179$ and P_0 either to the left or the right of the Skiba manifold, the result is approximately the same as the result for the reduced form of the lake. The adjustment in P to either the oligotrophic or eutrophic regime of the lake is fast, followed by slow adjustments in M and thus P, along the isocline $\dot{P} = 0$. For higher initial conditions M_0, the pattern is the same, but the adjustment process to one of the steady states takes longer. Furthermore, lowering the parameter γ further yields a bifurcation back to one steady state, but this steady state is in the eutrophic regime of the lake. A mirror picture results when compared to the case for a high γ, with a weak Skiba manifold again for high initial conditions M_0.

In the case of n polluters, analysis of the cooperative solution and the noncooperative equilibria follows the same route as in Sections 3.4 and 3.5. The cooperative solution coincides with the optimal management solution, independent of the number of polluters n. The necessary conditions for the open-loop Nash equilibrium with parameter γ coincide with the necessary conditions for the optimal management solution with parameter γ/n. The open-loop Nash equilibrium for $n = 2$ is not unique and leads to a pollution trap. The extension of the Markov perfect equilibrium in the Section 3.5 to fast and slow dynamics is still open for research. It requires a serious computational effort, and the question is if the additional effort will lead to more insights. On the other hand, the software for these types of problems will become available soon, and then it will be relatively easy to perform these analyses and to see what it provides.

3.6 Stable Agreements in a Simple Game

The analysis in the previous sections on cooperation versus noncooperation in the management of ecosystems with tipping points has interesting aspects. It was shown that for favourable initial conditions and (if needed) some coordination, the open-loop Nash equilibrium for $\gamma = 1$ and $n = 2$ moves the lake to the oligotrophic regime. Furthermore, the Markov perfect equilibrium always moves the lake out of the eutrophic regime. However, cooperation dominates these outcomes, of course, in terms of the value of the objective. If the lake is situated within one jurisdiction, the government can try to regulate the way the lake is used with taxes, but as was seen in the previous sections, a tax that can easily be implemented does not work well. It becomes even more complicated for the global management of ecosystems, such as the climate system or the fisheries on the high seas, where voluntary cooperation between countries is required.

The problem is that each economic agent has an incentive to deviate from the cooperative solution. The literature on international environmental agreements introduced a concept from cartel theory (d'Aspremont et al., 1983), where the incentive to cooperate and the incentive to deviate balance in a partial agreement or a stable coalition (Hoel, 1992; Carraro and Siniscalco, 1993; Barrett, 1994). When the concept of a tipping point arose, the literature focused on the question whether a Nash equilibrium can avoid tipping if it is optimal to do so (Barrett, 2013). In that paper, tipping simply implies a fixed loss and depending on this loss, a Nash equilibrium may exist that avoids tipping. This section takes this analysis one step further and shows when a stable coalition avoids tipping (Wagener and de Zeeuw, 2021). The economic agents are countries trying to strike an international environmental agreement. This section analyzes the issue for a simple model with abatement as decision variable and a fixed loss. Section 3.8 extends the method to the lake game of Section 3.3. In Section 3.8, also the question is considered whether a Nash equilibrium or a stable coalition exists that induces the ecosystem to tip back, after tipping has occurred.

Abatement is the general term for all the actions that reduce the emissions that damage the natural environment. A certain critical level of abatement $\hat{q}$ is needed to avoid tipping. Suppose that n countries choose abatement levels $q_i, i = 1, 2, \ldots, n$, with cost functions $C_i(q_i) = 0.5\gamma q_i^2$ and benefit functions $B_i(q) = \beta q$, where q denotes total abatement. Without loss of generality, the parameters can be normalized to $\gamma = \beta = 1$. When the countries ignore the tipping point, the full cooperative solution is $q_i = n$ with total abatement $q = n^2$ and net benefits $0.5n^2$ for each country. The Nash equilibrium is $q_i = 1$ with total abatement $q = n$ and net benefits $n - 0.5$ for each country. This is a prisoner's dilemma: When the countries cooperate, each country has an incentive to deviate and to choose $q_i = 1$ because its net benefits are larger, that is, $(n-1)n + 0.5 > 0.5n^2$ for $n > 1$. Moreover, partial cooperation is only stable for very small coalitions. For a coalition of size m, so that there are $n - m$ outsiders, total abatement becomes $q = m^2 + n - m$. A coalition member has net benefits $m^2 + n - m - 0.5m^2$, and an outsider has net benefits $m^2 + n - m - 0.5$. A coalition member does not have an incentive to leave if its net benefits are not smaller than the net benefits as an outsider to a coalition of size $m - 1$, that is, if $0.5m^2 + n - m$ is at least $(m-1)^2 + n - (m-1) - 0.5$. This holds if $0.5m^2 - 2m + 1.5 \leq 0$ or $(m-1)(m-3) \leq 0$. It follows that the only stable coalitions are coalitions with size $m = 2$ or $m = 3$. This is the usual grim story for a prisoner's dilemma.

The n countries must abate up to the critical level $\hat{q}$ to avoid tipping. If total abatement q stays below this critical level $\hat{q}$, tipping occurs and yields a loss of welfare l for each country. It follows that the benefit functions become $B_i(q) = q - l$, if $q < \hat{q}$, and $B_i(q) = q$, if $q \geq \hat{q}$. If the countries cooperate and total abatement $n^2 > \hat{q}$, tipping will not occur, so that they do not have to consider increasing abatement. However, if $n^2 < \hat{q}$, tipping occurs, and net benefits are $0.5n^2 - l$ for each country, which yields the trade-off. Either the countries abate up to the critical level $\hat{q}$ or they let tipping occur and accept the welfare loss l for each country. Assuming symmetry, each country abates $\hat{q}/n$ if they choose $\hat{q}$. It is better for the countries collectively to abate up to the level $\hat{q}$

if the net benefits for each country are higher than when they let tipping occur, that is,

$$\hat{q} - 0.5\left(\frac{\hat{q}}{n}\right)^2 > 0.5n^2 - l \Rightarrow l > 0.5\left(\frac{\hat{q}}{n} - n\right)^2, \tag{25}$$

or if the loss of welfare l is larger than the costs of the additional abatement.

If the countries do not cooperate and total abatement $n > \hat{q}$, tipping will not occur and there exists only one Nash equilibrium. However, if $n < \hat{q}$, tipping occurs, with net benefits $n - 0.5 - l$ for each country. The question now is whether $q_i = \hat{q}/n, i = 1, 2, \ldots, n$, is also a Nash equilibrium, so that a Nash equilibrium exists that avoids tipping. This requires that a country does not have an incentive to deviate in case the other countries choose abatement level $\hat{q}/n$. If a country deviates, it chooses abatement level $1 < \hat{q}/n$ with costs 0.5, and accepts the welfare loss l because tipping occurs. It is better for a country not to deviate if

$$\hat{q} - 0.5\left(\frac{\hat{q}}{n}\right)^2 > (n-1)\frac{\hat{q}}{n} + 1 - 0.5 - l \Rightarrow l > 0.5\left(\frac{\hat{q}}{n} - 1\right)^2. \tag{26}$$

It follows that if the welfare loss l is sufficiently high, the countries do not have to cooperate to avoid tipping but only need to coordinate on this Nash equilibrium. However, comparing Equation 26 with Equation 25 shows that it requires, of course, a larger welfare loss l to be able to rely on this option than the welfare loss that induces the countries to avoid tipping by cooperating.

For values of l where the first condition (Equation 25) holds but the second condition (Equation 26) does not hold, it is still collectively optimal to avoid tipping, but it cannot be achieved in a Nash equilibrium. The question is whether stable partial cooperation can avoid tipping in that case. Suppose that the members of a coalition of size m contribute $\hat{q}^m$ to the critical level of abatement and the outsiders contribute $\hat{q}^o$, so that $m\hat{q}^m + (n-m)\hat{q}^o = \hat{q}$. Given the contributions of the $n - m$ outsiders, the coalition has the choice to abate m^2 and let tipping occur, with costs $0.5m^2$ and welfare loss l for each member, or to have each member contribute the abatement level $\hat{q}^m$. It is better for the coalition to contribute, if the net benefits of each member are higher than when the coalition lets tipping occur, that is,

$$\hat{q} - 0.5(\hat{q}^m)^2 > (n-m)\hat{q}^o + 0.5m^2 - l \Rightarrow l > 0.5(\hat{q}^m - m)^2. \tag{27}$$

Similarly, given the contribution of the coalition and the other $n - m - 1$ outsiders, an outsider has the choice to abate 1 and let tipping occur, with costs 0.5 and welfare loss l, or to contribute the abatement level $\hat{q}^o$. It is better for the outsider to contribute, if the net benefits for this outsider are higher than when it lets tipping occur, that is,

$$\hat{q} - 0.5(\hat{q}^o)^2 > m\hat{q}^m + (n - m - 1)\hat{q}^o + 0.5 - l \Rightarrow l > 0.5(\hat{q}^o - 1)^2.$$
(28)

These conditions (Equations 27 and 28) both hold if $\hat{q}^m - m = \hat{q}^o - 1$. It follows that

$$\hat{q}^m = \frac{\hat{q}}{n} + \frac{(n-m)(m-1)}{n}, \quad \hat{q}^o = \frac{\hat{q}}{n} - \frac{m(m-1)}{n},$$
(29)

is a Nash equilibrium between the coalition of size m and the $n - m$ outsiders that avoids tipping, under the condition that the loss of welfare l satisfies

$$l > 0.5\left(\frac{\hat{q}}{n} - \frac{m^2 + n - m}{n}\right)^2.$$
(30)

This condition (Equation 30) becomes Equation 26 for $m = 1$ (Nash equilibrium) and Equation 25 for $m = n$ (cooperative outcome). Step by step, the gap between these conditions is filled by increasing the size m of the coalition. It means that a larger size of the coalition, or a higher level of cooperation, is needed to avoid tipping when the loss of welfare l is decreasing.

The question is whether these coalitions are stable. Suppose that the loss of welfare l is such that a coalition of size m is needed to avoid tipping. This means that if a country leaves the coalition, the remaining size of the coalition $m - 1$ is not large enough to avoid tipping. In this situation, the coalition chooses abatement level $(m - 1)^2$ and the outsiders abatement level 1, and each country has a loss of welfare l. Stability requires that a coalition member does not have an incentive to leave, which means that the net benefits of a member of a coalition of size m are not smaller than the net benefits of an outsider to a coalition of size $m - 1$, that is,

$$\hat{q} - 0.5(\hat{q}^m)^2 \geq (m - 1)^2 + n - m + 0.5 - l.$$
(31)

The lower bound of l, for which a coalition of size m avoids tipping, is given by the inequalities (Equations 27, 28 and 30). Denoting this lower bound by $\hat{l}$, so $\hat{l} = 0.5(\hat{q}^m - m)^2 = 0.5(\hat{q}^o - 1)^2$, and using $\hat{q} = m\hat{q}^m + (n - m)\hat{q}^o$, the stability condition Equation 31 can be rewritten as

$$(m - 1)(m - 3) \leq 2\left(l - \hat{l} + (n - m)\sqrt{2\hat{l}}\right).$$
(32)

The usual grim story has changed. It is possible now to have larger stable coalitions than coalitions with size $m = 2$ or $m = 3$. For example, suppose that the critical abatement level $\hat{q} = 150$, and the number of countries $n = 10$. Condition Equation 30 shows that in the range $48.02 < l < 60.5$, a coalition of size $m = 7$ is needed to avoid tipping, in the range $35.28 < l < 48.02$, a coalition of size $m = 8$, and in the range $23.12 < l < 35.28$, a coalition of size $m = 9$. Furthermore, condition Equation 32 shows that the coalition of size $m = 7$ is stable, the coalition of size $m = 8$ is stable for $l \geq 35.98$ but not for $l < 35.98$, and the coalition of size $m = 9$ is not stable anymore. At some point, the incentive to free ride and to accept tipping dominates the incentive to cooperate and to avoid tipping, because the level of cooperation is high and the loss of welfare l is low.

The gap between Equations 25 and 26 shows the values of the loss of welfare l for which it is collectively optimal to avoid tipping but for which this cannot be achieved in a Nash equilibrium. In the example, this range becomes $12.5 < l < 98$. For $l < 12.5$, it is better to let tipping occur, and for $l > 98$, a Nash equilibrium exists that avoids tipping. Stable partial cooperation covers a large part of this range, $35.98 < l < 98$, with coalitions up to size $m = 8$. For smaller values of l, a coalition of size $m = 8$, $m = 9$, or full cooperation is needed to avoid tipping, but these coalitions are not stable. The good news is, however, that the loss of welfare l is small.

Finally, the critical level of abatement $\hat{q}$ needed to avoid tipping is uncertain. An interesting result arises when considering this uncertainty. In a similar model, Barrett and Dannenberg (2012) show that the option to coordinate on a Nash equilibrium and avoid tipping disappears when the range of uncertainty becomes too large. They design an experiment to test in the lab whether the players indeed play a coordination game within this range but a prisoners' dilemma outside this range, and they find strong support for this theoretical result.

3.7 Stable Agreements in the Lake Game

This section extends the analysis of Section 3.6 to the lake game. Note that the decision variables are emissions or loadings of phosphorus now, and not abatement. After tipping, the loss is not fixed, but the polluters optimize or move to the Nash equilibrium in the eutrophic regime. It also considers the question whether a Nash equilibrium or stable coalition exists that results in the lake tipping back to the oligotrophic regime. Section 3.3 derives the necessary condition Equation 14 for the full cooperative problem, given by Equations 9 and 10, and the necessary condition Equation 19 for the individual open-loop Nash equilibrium, given by Equation 15. The open-loop Nash equilibrium between the coalition of size m and the $n - m$ outsiders requires to simultaneously solve the problems

$$\max_{a_1(.),\dots,a_m(.)} \int_0^\infty e^{-\rho t}\left[\sum_{i=1}^m \ln a_i(t) - m\gamma x^2(t)\right] dt,$$

$$\max_{a_i(.)} \int_0^\infty e^{-\rho t}[\ln a_i(t) - \gamma x^2(t)]dt, i = m+1,\dots,n, \tag{33}$$

subject to (10). The current-value Hamiltonian functions become

$$H(x, a_1,\dots,a_m,\lambda) = \sum_{i=1}^m \ln a_i - m\gamma x^2 + \lambda\left(\sum_{i=1}^m a_i + \sum_{i=m+1}^n a_i - bx + \frac{x^2}{x^2+1}\right),$$

$$H_i(x, a_i,\lambda_i) = \ln a_i - \gamma x^2 + \lambda_i\left(a_i + \sum_{j\neq i}^n a_j - bx + \frac{x^2}{x^2+1}\right), i=m+1,\dots,n,$$

$$\tag{34}$$

and the necessary conditions become Equation 10 and

$$\lambda = -\frac{1}{a_i}, i = 1, 2,\dots, m, \dot\lambda(t) = \left(\rho + b - \frac{2x(t)}{\left(x^2(t)+1\right)^2}\right)\lambda(t) + 2m\gamma x(t),$$

$$\lambda_i = -\frac{1}{a_i}, \dot\lambda_i(t) = \left(\rho + b - \frac{2x(t)}{\left(x^2(t)+1\right)^2}\right)\lambda_i(t) + 2\gamma x(t), i = m+1,\dots,n.$$

$$\tag{35}$$

It follows that $\lambda = m\lambda_i$, so that $\sum_{i=1}^m a_i = -\frac{1}{\lambda_i}$, and

$$\dot a(t) = -\left(\rho + b - \frac{2x(t)}{\left(x^2(t)+1\right)^2}\right)a(t) + 2\frac{\gamma}{n-m+1}x(t)a^2(t), a = \sum_{i=1}^n a_i.$$

$$\tag{36}$$

Equation 36 is the same as Equation 19 for the individual Nash equilibrium, but for $n - m + 1$ polluters. For these specific objective functionals, the coalition acts as an individual polluter. For $m = n$, Equation 36 is the same as Equation 14 for the cooperative outcome.

The main idea in Section 3.3 is to show that for given values of the parameters b for the lake, so that tipping and hysteresis can occur, and ρ for the discount rate, the lake can end up in either the oligotrophic or the eutrophic regime of the lake. More specifically, if the cost parameter $\gamma = 1$, it is optimal to move the lake to the oligotrophic regime but if the cost parameter $\gamma = 0.5$, or if the number of polluters $n = 2$, it depends on the initial condition x_0 of the stock of phosphorus in the lake. Optimal management for $\gamma = 0.5$ yields a Skiba or indifference point $\bar{x}_0$, which means that for the initial conditions below (above) this point, it is optimal to move the lake to the oligotrophic (eutrophic) regime. For the open-loop Nash equilibrium with $n = 2$, a similar split arises but with a range of initial conditions where the Nash equilibrium is not unique. In that range, coordination between the polluters on the right Nash equilibrium can move the lake to the oligotrophic regime, so that this regime can be reached for a larger set of initial conditions than for optimal management with $\gamma = 0.5$. Above this range, however, only one Nash equilibrium exists that moves the lake to the eutrophic regime.

This section turns the analysis around. For a given initial condition x_0 of the stock of phosphorus in the oligotrophic regime of the lake, the first question is for which values of the cost parameter γ the lake does not tip and stays in the oligotrophic regime. When analyzing the full lake model, Section 3.5 already briefly mentions that lowering the parameter γ further (meaning that the loss of ecosystem services has a low weight in the objective functional) yields a bifurcation back to one steady state, with this steady state in the eutrophic regime of the lake. Indeed, given $x_0 = 0$, a value $\hat{\gamma}$ exists so that for $\gamma > \hat{\gamma}$, it is optimal to move the lake to the steady state in the oligotrophic regime, but for $\gamma < \hat{\gamma}$, it is optimal to let the lake tip and move it to the steady state in the eutrophic regime (Wagener, 2003). For the open-loop Nash equilibrium with n polluters, the question arises for which values of the cost parameter γ a Nash equilibrium exists that avoids tipping and keeps the lake in the oligotrophic regime (see also Diekert, 2017). A value $\bar{\gamma}$ exists so that for $\gamma > \bar{\gamma}$, a Nash equilibrium exists that moves the lake to the candidate Nash equilibrium steady state in the oligotrophic regime of the lake (Wagener and de Zeeuw, 2021). The costs of tipping are sufficiently high now, so that there is no individual incentive to deviate and move to the eutrophic regime. For $\gamma < \bar{\gamma}$, the only Nash equilibrium is the one that tips and moves the lake to the Nash equilibrium steady state in the eutrophic regime of the lake. The welfare implications can be substantial. For example, for the parameter values $b = 0.6$, $\rho = 0.03$, $n = 2$, and $x_0 = 0$, these critical values are $\hat{\gamma} = 0.43$ for cooperation and $\bar{\gamma} = 0.66$ for noncooperation. It follows that for $0.43 < \gamma < 0.66$, cooperation is needed to avoid tipping and to keep the lake in the oligotrophic regime. If $\gamma = 0.7$, however, the polluters can coordinate on the Nash equilibrium that avoids tipping, leading to the net individual welfare -100.38, just below the optimal welfare -100.24, a drop of only 0.1%. On the other hand, if $\gamma = 0.6$, only one Nash equilibrium exists that moves the lake to the eutrophic regime, leading to the net individual welfare -120.13, far below the optimal welfare -99.8. The gains of cooperation are large now, almost 17%.

The critical value $\bar{y}$ depends on the number of polluters n. This implies that critical values arise for the open-loop Nash equilibrium between the coalition of size m and $n - m$ outsiders as well, because this is the same problem as the open-loop Nash equilibrium with $n - m + 1$ polluters. The critical value $\bar{y}$ is increasing in the total number of polluters n because it requires larger costs of tipping to suppress the individual incentive to deviate when the number of polluters is high. This implies that the critical values in the case of partial cooperation are decreasing in the number of coalition members m. Fixing the number of polluters n, and denoting these critical values as a function of the number of coalition members by $y(m)$, it follows that $y(1) = \bar{y}$ and $y(n) = \hat{y}$. By increasing the number of coalition members, this function fills the gap between the critical value $\bar{y}$ for the existence of a Nash equilibrium that avoids tipping and the critical value $\hat{y}$ for optimal management that avoids tipping. The next question is whether the coalitions of size m, which are needed to avoid tipping, are stable. The calculations require advanced numerical methods, but the pattern of the results is the same as in Section 3.6. It is possible to avoid tipping for a large range of values for the cost parameter y, and the stable coalitions are larger than in the case without the possibility of tipping, because the balance between the incentive to cooperate and the incentive to deviate changes (see also Miller and Nkuiya, 2016). Figure 5 shows the result for $n = 10$.

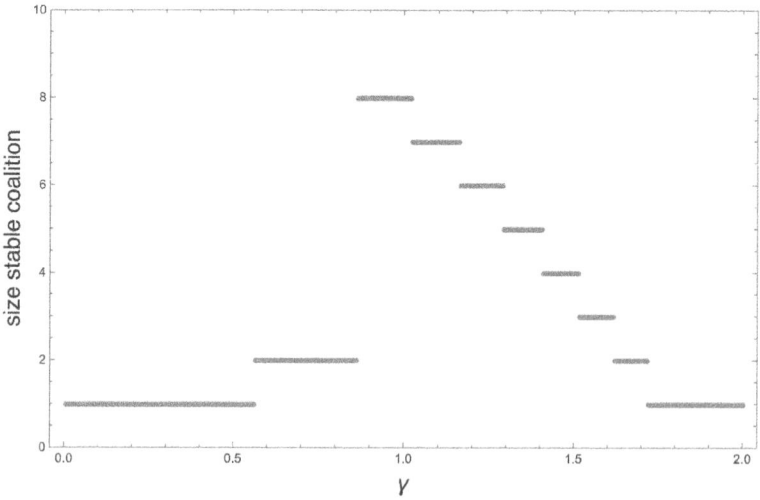

Figure 5 Stable coalition size avoiding tipping.

Figure 5 implies that for $\gamma > \bar{\gamma} = 1.69$, the polluters can coordinate on the Nash equilibrium that avoids tipping. For $1.58 < \gamma < 1.69$, a coalition of size $m = 2$ is needed to avoid tipping, and this coalition is stable. Lowering the cost parameter γ further requires, step by step, a larger coalition to avoid tipping. These coalitions are stable up to $m = 8$. For $\gamma < 0.88$, larger coalitions are needed to avoid tipping, but these are not stable. Below some value, it is also not optimal anymore to avoid tipping. For these values of the cost parameter γ, the usual story applies. In this specific case, for $0.58 < \gamma < 0.88$, the largest stable coalition is $m = 2$, and for $\gamma < 0.58$, stable partial cooperation is not possible. The conclusion is again, as in Section 3.6, that for a large range of values of the cost parameter γ, that is, $0.88 < \gamma < 1.69$, stable partial cooperation avoids tipping and if this is not possible, the costs of tipping are low. The story is not so grim anymore.

If tipping of the lake has already occurred, and the lake is in the eutrophic regime, the question is now whether stable coalitions can induce the lake tipping back to the oligotrophic regime. Figure 6 shows the result.

Note that the critical value for the cost parameter γ below which partial cooperation is needed to induce tipping back is much larger than the corresponding critical value in Figure 5. The costs of being in the eutrophic regime of the lake must be high to have a Nash equilibrium that moves the lake back to the oligotrophic regime. The numbers in Figure 6 result by taking the initial condition of the stock of phosphorus $x_0 = 1.75$. The pattern is the same again. Lowering the cost parameter γ requires, step by step, a larger coalition to induce

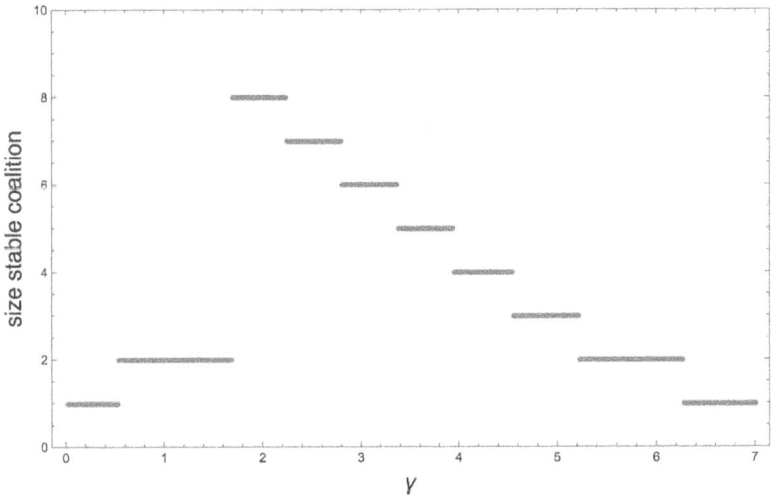

Figure 6 Stable coalition size inducing tipping back.

tipping back. These coalitions are stable up to $m = 8$. The coalitions of size $m = 9$ and $m = 10$ are not stable but in these cases, it is still optimal to tip the lake back. This implies that for these values of the cost parameter γ, tipping is physically reversible (because $b = 0.6$) but socially irreversible, because these large coalitions are not stable. It is interesting to note that for $\gamma = 2$, a coalition of size $m = 8$ is needed to get out of the eutrophic regime, but Figure 5 shows that for $\gamma = 2$, coordination on the Nash equilibrium is sufficient to avoid tipping again. This means that a high level of cooperation is needed to push the system from a "brown" to a "green" regime (from green to blue in the case of the lake) but only coordination is needed to keep the system in the favorable regime. Acemoglu et al. (2012) have a similar result where they show that only temporary policies are needed to redirect the innovation toward clean inputs for production.

3.8 Concluding Remarks

Section 3 provides different analyses of managing the lake system, except for Section 3.6, which provides the analysis of stable partial cooperation in a simpler model first. Section 3.1 introduces the lake model. Section 3.2 presents optimal management of the reduced form of the lake model and focuses on the existence of a Skiba point that separates the initial conditions ending up in the oligotrophic or eutrophic regime of the lake. Sections 3.3 and 3.4 derive the open-loop Nash and the Markov perfect equilibrium in case of common property of the lake and noncooperative behavior. The multiplicity of Markov perfect equilibria gives the opportunity to choose a Nash equilibrium that moves the lake out of the eutrophic regime and close to the optimal management steady state. Section 3.5 returns to the full lake model and shows the existence of weak Skiba manifolds that separate initial conditions ending up in the same steady state but following a different trajectory. Section 3.7 shows the results for stable partial cooperation. In the presence of tipping points, it is possible to form large stable coalitions that avoid tipping or induce tipping back.

This Element chooses to present the different techniques in detail and use these techniques only to analyze the lake model instead of reviewing the application of these techniques to several models. The lake model is a metaphor for many ecological systems with tipping points. Understanding the mechanisms and the results for the lake model provides a framework for analyzing other ecological models with tipping points. The main messages of Section 3 are twofold. First, it is important to restrict pollution to avoid tipping or to avoid passing the Skiba point and ending up in the eutrophic regime of the lake.

Second, the possibility of tipping allows for a higher level of cooperation, so that not all the results in Section 3 are warnings for bad outcomes.

The lake model is developed by limnologists and is used for simulations to show the problems that can occur by continuing the loading of phosphorus on the lake. This section turned the loading of phosphorus into a control variable to show the optimal management of the lake and the outcomes that result for different levels and different forms of cooperation between the users of the lake. The lake model, however, is simple and represents only a small part of the larger ecosystem. It requires the input of other ecologists and hydrogeologists to deepen and extend the modelling, and to apply economics to the larger ecosystem. This Element describes a first step in the interdisciplinary work between economists and ecologists, but further interaction is needed to move the work forward. It requires mutual understanding of what the different disciplines can contribute, but the analysis of the lake model shows that this is possible and fruitful.

4 The Risk of Tipping

Section 3 focuses on ecological models with tipping points, where the economics is restricted to a welfare indicator balancing the benefits of polluting economic activities and the costs of polluting the ecological system. This section focuses on economic models with parameters representing the natural environment, where the parameters can shift due to tipping in the natural environment. For example, the carrying capacity in a fishery can shift due to a tipping point in the ecological system to which the fish belongs, or the total factor productivity in an economy can shift due to a climate tipping point. A shift in a parameter implies a change in the structure, dynamics, and equilibria of the economic system, which is an essential characteristic of tipping. In general, a shift means a loss of productivity. When the natural environment cannot be precisely modelled, tipping becomes just an uncertain event at a point T in time, and economic management must take account of the risk of tipping. The uncertainty is captured by the hazard rate, which can be exogenous or endogenous. Endogenous means that the hazard rate depends on the economic activities.

Hazard rates are not new in economic analysis (Kamien and Schwartz, 1971; Cropper, 1976) but they usually apply to a possible collapse in stock or utility. In the case of the use of resources, for example, the possibility of such a collapse is an incentive for increased exploitation. In this setting, the hazard rate has the same effect as the discount rate, where an increase in mortality risk increases an individual's discount rate. If the hazard rate is endogenous, increased exploitation increases the hazard rate and the possibility of collapse, and thus has an opposite effect in optimal management. The outcome is ambiguous. This approach was used to analyze the optimal management of forests subject to fire (Reed, 1984), fisheries subject to collapse (Reed, 1988), and environmental pollution (Clarke and Reed, 1994). Similar analyses on the optimal management of environmental pollution (Tsur and Zemel, 1998) and climate change (Tsur and Zemel, 1996; Gjerde et al., 1999; Keller et al., 2004) have uncertain thresholds, and in these cases, tipping triggers a discontinuous decline in the stock variable or in the value function. The approach in this section is to model tipping as a sudden shift in the system dynamics, which is more in line with the ecological literature on tipping points. Taking account of optimal management of the system with lower productivity after tipping also implies a lower value function, but the effect on the problem before tipping is different from the effect of assuming a sudden fixed loss, as in the earlier literature. This will become clear in the analysis that follows. Section 4.1 starts with some technical preliminaries. Sections 4.2–4.4 apply the results to a fishery model where tipping in the ecosystem yields a shock to the carrying capacity (Polasky et al., 2011). Sections 4.5–4.7 analyze the Ramsey growth model where climate tipping causes a shock to the total factor productivity (van der Ploeg and de Zeeuw, 2019).

4.1 Technical Preliminaries

The hazard rate $h(t)$ is the limit for $\Delta t \to 0$ of the conditional probability that tipping at T occurs between t and $t + \Delta t$, and not before t, divided by Δt. Formally,

$$h(t) = \lim_{\Delta t \to 0} \frac{\Pr[T \in (t, t + \Delta t) | T \notin (0, t)]}{\Delta t}. \tag{37}$$

It follows that this conditional probability can be approximated by $h(t)\Delta t$, which will prove to be useful in deriving the following results. For a constant hazard rate h, the probability distribution for the tipping point T has the exponential density function he^{-ht} (with mean $1/h$), and therefore, the cumulative density function $1 - e^{-ht}$ (a Poisson process). It follows that the probability of survival is e^{-ht}. If the hazard rate is not constant, ht becomes $\int_0^t h(\tau)d\tau$.

Both Pontryagin's maximum principle and dynamic programming can be used to solve the problem of optimal management. In case of a differential game, the outcomes are different (as was seen in Sections 3.3 and 3.4) but for optimal management, it is a matter of choice what suits better. In the presence of a potential tipping point, driven by the hazard rate, it is convenient to start the analysis with dynamic programming. The problem splits into a Hamilton–Jacobi–Bellman equation in the current-value function after tipping (with a shift in the parameter) and one before tipping that takes account of the possibility of tipping. The crux of this approach is that the stochastic optimization problem before tipping with an uncertain finite horizon and a scrap value turns into a deterministic optimization problem with an infinite horizon (Reed, 1988). It is also possible to use Pontrygin's maximum principle from the start (Gjerde et al., 1999), but the analysis becomes more complicated and less intuitive. The solution path of the problem with an infinite horizon before tipping is valid until tipping occurs, and then it switches to the solution path after tipping.

Suppose that the basic optimal management problem is given by

$$\max_{u(.)} \int_0^\infty e^{-\rho t} B(z(t), u(t)) \qquad \dot{z}(t) = f(z(t), u(t)), z(0) = z_0, \tag{38}$$

where B is an objective function, like net benefits, profit, or utility, f is a state-transition function, z is a stock, like a resource stock, a capital stock or a pollution stock, u is an action, like harvest or consumption, ρ is the discount rate, and z_0 is the initial condition.

Tipping in the sense of a structural change in the dynamics of the system means that the function f switches from f_b before tipping to f_a after tipping. The optimization problem after tipping is standard. Note that the problem is stationary, because the objective function and the state-transition function do not explicitly depend on time. Using dynamic programming, the current-value function V_a must satisfy the Hamilton–Jacobi–Bellman equation

$$\rho V_a(z) = \max_u [B(z, u) + V_a'(z) f_a(z, u)]. \tag{39}$$

It is somewhat tedious but straightforward to derive the Hamilton–Jacobi–Bellman equation before tipping (Reed, 1988; Polasky et al., 2011). The value function W_b is the maximal expected value of the welfare indicator at time t for the stock $z(t)$. Tipping implies a switch to the value function after tipping, and the hazard rate h implies that $h\Delta t$ approximates the conditional probability that tipping occurs between t and $t + \Delta t$, and not before t. It follows that

$$W_b(t, z(t)) = \max_{u(.)} \left[\int_t^{t+\Delta t} e^{-\rho \tau} B(z(\tau), u(\tau)) d\tau + \right.$$
$$\left. (1 - h\Delta t) W_b(t + \Delta t, z(t + \Delta t)) + h\Delta t e^{-\rho(t+\Delta t)} V_a(z(t + \Delta t)) \right]. \tag{40}$$

For small Δt, $e^{-\rho t} B\Big(z(t), u(t)\Big) \Delta t$ approximates the integral. Dividing by Δt yields

$$0 = \max_{u(.)} \Big[e^{-\rho t} B\Big(z(t), u(t)\Big) - h\Big(W_b\Big(t + \Delta t, z(t + \Delta t)\Big)$$

$$+ e^{-\rho(t + \Delta t)} V_a\Big(z(t + \Delta t)\Big)\Big) + \Big(W_b\Big(t + \Delta t, z(t + \Delta t)\Big) - W_b\Big(t, z(t)\Big)\Big) / \Delta t\Big].$$

$$(41)$$

Assuming that W_b is differentiable in (t, z), the last term in Equation 41 becomes $W_{bt} + W_{bz}\dot{z}$ if $\Delta t \rightarrow 0$. It follows that taking the limit for $\Delta t \rightarrow 0$, yields

$$0 = \max_{u(t)} \Big[e^{-\rho t} B\Big(z(t), u(t)\Big) - h\Big(W_b\Big(t, z(t)\Big) - e^{-\rho t} V_a\Big(z(t)\Big)\Big)$$

$$+ W_{bt}\Big(t, z(t)\Big) + W_{bz}\Big(t, z(t)\Big) f_b\Big(z(t), u(t)\Big)\Big].$$

$$(42)$$

Multiplying Equation 42 by $e^{\rho t}$ and introducing the current-value function $V_b(t, z) = e^{\rho t} W_b(t, z)$ (with $V_{bt} = \rho V_b + e^{\rho t} W_{bt}$, $V_{bz} = e^{\rho t} W_{bz}$) turns Equation 42 into a stationary equation, so that V_b depends only on z, and $V_{bt} = 0$. This yields the Hamilton–Jacobi–Bellman equation before tipping

$$\rho V_b(z) = \max_u [B(z, u) - h\Big(V_b(z) - V_a(z)\Big) + V_b'(z) f_b(z, u)].$$

$$(43)$$

This is also the Hamilton–Jacobi–Bellman equation for the deterministic optimization problem with infinite horizon and a loss function $h\Big(V_b(z) - V_a(z)\Big)$, which is the risk of tipping into a regime with the lower current value $V_a < V_b$. Equation 43 has the state-transition function f_b instead of the f_a that appears in the Hamilton–Jacobi–Bellman equation after tipping (Equation 39). The solution procedure starts by solving Equation 39 for $V_a(z)$, followed by solving Equation 43.

4.2 The Fishery

Research on many fisheries all over the world has shown that the logistic growth model (Verhulst, 1838) captures the growth of a fish stock quite well. Logistic growth starts with low growth when the stock of fish s is small, then accelerates, and then levels off and converges to a maximum level $\hat{s}$ because of lack of food or other resources. The level $\hat{s}$ is the maximum level of the fish stock that the ecological system to which this fish belongs can sustain. This level is called the carrying capacity. The logistic growth curve is the solution of the differential equation

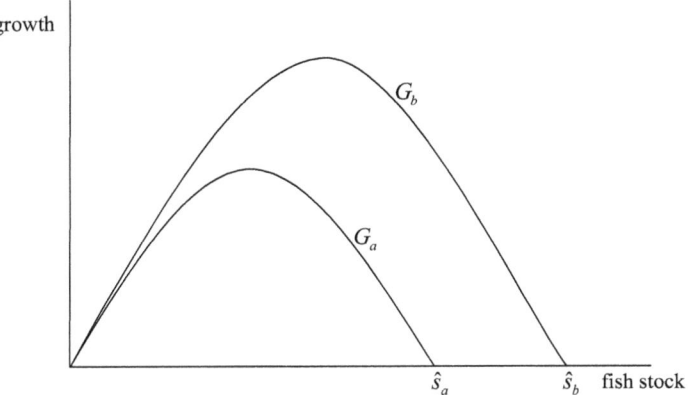

Figure 7 Tipping in a fishery.

$$\dot{s}(t) = G\Big(s(t)\Big), G = gs(1 - s/\hat{s}), s(0) = s_0, \tag{44}$$

where G denotes the growth function, g the growth rate, and s_0 the initial fish stock. When the fish stock is small, the term between brackets in the growth function G is close to 1 and the model behaves like a standard growth model, with initially low growth. When the fish stock is close to the carrying capacity $\hat{s}$, this term is close to 0, and growth is also low. In between, growth is high. Tipping in the ecological system to which the fish belongs implies a shock to the growth rate g or to the carrying capacity $\hat{s}$. Figure 7 shows the effect on the growth function G of a shift in the carrying capacity from $\hat{s}_b$ to $\hat{s}_a$. The growth function shifts from G_b to G_a.

If a unit of fish sells at a fixed price π on the market, and if the costs of fishing are 0, the basic optimal management problem of the fishery is given by

$$\max_{y(\,)} \int_0^\infty e^{-\rho t}\pi y(t)dt,$$

$$\dot{s}(t) = G\Big(s(t)\Big) - y(t), G(s) = gs(1 - s/\hat{s}), s(0) = s_0, \tag{45}$$

where y denotes the harvest of fish.

The solution to this linear optimal management problem is well-known (e.g., Clark, 1990). The solution is to take the most rapid approach path toward the steady-state fish stock s^*, which is given by the golden rule $G'(s^*) = \rho$. This implies a moratorium on fishing when $s_0 < s^*$, and maximal harvesting when $s_0 > s^*$, until the steady state is reached where harvesting becomes $y = G(s^*)$.

Section 4.1 shows that the Hamilton–Jacobi–Bellman equations (with hazard rate $h(s)$) become

$$\rho V_a(s) = \max_{y} \left[\pi y + V_a{}'(s)\big(G_a(s) - y\big) \right],$$

$$\rho V_b(s) = \max_{y} \left[\pi y - h(s)\big(V_b(s) - V_a(s)\big) + V_b{}'(s)\big(G_b(s) - y\big) \right]. \quad (46)$$

After tipping, the first equation of Equation 46 applies and this is the standard fishery problem. Indeed, it shows that harvest $y = 0$ if $\pi < V_a{}'(s)$, and harvest y is maximal if $\pi > V_a{}'(s)$. In the steady-state stock s_a, harvest $y = G_a(s_a)$ and the marginal value $V_a{}'(s_a)$ is equal to the price π. For $s < s_a$, harvest $y = 0$, and the first equation of Equation 46 becomes $\rho V_a(s) = V_a{}'(s)G_a(s)$. Differentiation with respect to s yields $V_a{}''(s)G_a(s) = \left(\rho - G_a{}'(s) \right) V_a{}'(s)$. For $s > s_a$, harvest y is maximal $y = y^m$, and the first equation of Equation 46 becomes $\rho V_a(s) = \pi y^m + V_a{}'(s)\big(G_a(s) - y^m\big)$. Differentiation with respect to s yields $V_a{}''(s)\big(G_a(s) - y^m\big) = \left(\rho - G_a{}'(s) \right) V_a{}'(s)$. It follows that the steady-state fish stock s_a is given by the golden rule $G_a{}'(s_a) = \rho$. For $s < s_a$, the fish stock s increases, $G_a{}'(s) > \rho$, and $V_a{}''(s) < 0$, so that the marginal value $V_a{}'(s)$ decreases. For $s > s_a$, the fish stock s decreases, $G_a{}'(s) < \rho$, and $V_a{}''(s) < 0$, so that for the decreasing fish stock s in this area, the marginal value $V_a{}'(s)$ increases. For the steady-state stock s_a, harvest $y = G_a(s_a)$, $V_a{}''(s_a) = 0$, and the marginal value $V_a{}'(s_a) = \pi$. If the steady-state stock before tipping s_b is higher than the steady-state stock after tipping s_a (which is to be expected since the fishery conditions before tipping are better), and if it is possible to harvest the difference $y = s_b - s_a$ at once at the price π, $V_a{}'(s_b) = \pi$. Optimal management of the fishery can wait until tipping occurs and can then adjust immediately from the steady-state stock before tipping s_b to the steady-state stock after tipping s_a.

Before tipping the second equation of Equation 46 applies. The analysis is basically the same as for the optimization problem after tipping, but it has a different golden rule (Polasky et al., 2011). Harvest $y = 0$, if $\pi < V_b{}'(s)$, and harvest y is maximal, if $\pi > V_b{}'(s)$. In the steady-state stock s_b, harvest $y = G_b(s_b)$ and the marginal value $V_b{}'(s_b)$ is equal to the price π. For $s < s_b$, harvest $y = 0$, and for $s > s_b$, harvest y is maximal $y = y^m$. Differentiation of the resulting second equation of Equation 46 for $s < s_b$ and $s > s_b$, respectively, yields

$$V_b{}''(s)G_b(s) = v(s), s < s_b; \quad V_b{}''(s)\big(G_b(s) - y^m\big) = v(s), s > s_b,$$
$$v(s) = \left(\rho + h(s) - G_b{}'(s) \right) V_b{}'(s) - h(s)V_a{}'(s) + h'(s)\big(V_b(s) - V_a(s)\big).$$
$$(47)$$

It is not generally true that $v(s) < 0$ for $s < s_b$ and $v(s) > 0$ for $s > s_b$, as in the case after tipping.

The analysis becomes difficult but if a range exists where these inequalities hold, the golden rule that gives the steady-state fish stock s_b follows from $v(s) = 0$ in the second equation of Equation 47. Note from the second equation in Equation 46 with $y = 0$ that in the steady-state fish stock s_b

$$V_b'(s_b) = \pi, \, V_b(s_b) = \frac{\pi G_b(s_b) + h(s_b)V_a(s_b)}{\rho + h(s_b)}. \tag{48}$$

It follows that the golden rule becomes

$$G_b'(s_b) = \rho + h(s_b)\left(1 - \frac{V_a'(s_b)}{\pi}\right) + \frac{h'(s_b)}{\rho + h(s_b)}\left(G_b(s_b) - \frac{\rho V_a(s_b)}{\pi}\right). \tag{49}$$

It is time to draw some conclusions and to return to the point raised in the beginning of this section, where it was announced that the effect of a structural change in the system dynamics at a tipping point differs from the effect of a possible collapse in stock or utility. Note that a total collapse in stock or utility implies that $V_a(s) = 0$. Four cases are considered by also distinguishing a constant or exogenous hazard rate h versus an endogenous hazard rate $h(s)$, with $h'(s) < 0$.

Case 1: Exogenous hazard rate with stock collapse

In this case, the golden rule (Equation 49) becomes $G_b'(s_b) = \rho + h$. The hazard rate h adds to the discount rate ρ, and this leads to increased exploitation and a lower steady-state fish stock s_b.

Case 2: Endogenous hazard rate with stock collapse

In this case, the golden rule (Equation 49) becomes

$$G_b'(s_b) = \rho + h(s_b) + \frac{h'(s_b)}{\rho + h(s_b)} G_b(s_b). \tag{50}$$

The effect on the steady-state fish stock s_b is ambiguous. The first two terms at the right-hand side of Equation 50 show an increase in the discount rate, which leads to an increased exploitation, but the third term is negative (because $h'(s_b) < 0$), which has the opposite effect. A higher steady-state fish stock lowers the hazard rate, and thus the possibility of tipping. This ambiguity is the typical result in the literature that was discussed in the beginning of this section.

Case 3: Exogenous hazard rate with a change in system dynamics

In this case, the golden rule (Equation 49) becomes $G_b'(s_b) = \rho$, because $V_a'(s_b) = \pi$ under the assumption that it is possible to harvest the difference

$y = s_b - s_a$ at once at the price π. Optimal management of the fishery behaves as if there is no risk of tipping and adjusts to the new condition when tipping occurs. The steady-state fish stock s_b is the same as in the absence of tipping.

Case 4: Endogenous hazard rate with a change in system dynamics

In this case, the golden rule (Equation 49) becomes

$$G_b'(s_b) = \rho + \frac{h'(s_b)}{\rho + h(s_b)}\left(G_b(s_b) - \frac{\rho V_a(s_b)}{\pi}\right). \tag{51}$$

The second term at the right-hand side of Equation 51 is negative because $h'(s_b) < 0$ and because the value $\pi G_b(s_b)/\rho$ under the conditions before tipping is larger than the value $V_a(s_b)$ under the conditions after tipping. It follows that the steady-state fish stock s_b is higher than in the absence of tipping. The risk of tipping implies precautionary behavior.

The conclusion is that if tipping means a change in the system dynamics or a shift in a parameter of the ecological system such as the carrying capacity in the fishery, optimal management does not change if the potential tipping is exogenous but becomes precautionary if the probability of tipping is lower for a higher fish stock. The last situation accords with the famous *precautionary principle* and the earlier analysis gives a rigorous justification for this (compare Gollier and Treich, 2003). The standard fishery model is linear, and the analysis relies on the possibility of an instantaneous adjustment in the steady-state fish stock after tipping. Section 4.3 considers a more general nonlinear utility of harvest and shows that a constant hazard rate can then lead to precaution as well, but this depends on the value of the intertemporal utility parameter.

4.3 The Fishery Extended

The conclusion on precaution in the fishery with potential tipping is different in the case of a more general utility of harvest (Ren and Polasky, 2014; de Zeeuw and He, 2017). In Section 4.2, a constant hazard rate h leads to the same behavior as in the absence of tipping, and precautionary behavior results for an endogenous hazard rate $h(s)$. However, precautionary behavior can also result for a constant hazard rate if the price π is not constant and a more general utility of harvest applies. A switch to a more general welfare function also makes sense if the fishery is viewed as a metaphor for a general environmental economics problem where logistic growth applies because of the limited carrying capacity of the ecological system.

The basic optimal management problem of the fishery (Equation 45), for a more general welfare function, where U denotes the utility of harvest y, changes into

$$\max_{y(.)} \int_0^\infty e^{-\rho t} U\Big(y(t)\Big) \, dt,$$

$$\dot{s}(t) = G\Big(s(t)\Big) - y(t), G(s) = gs(1 - s/\hat{s}), s(0) = s_0. \tag{52}$$

The Hamilton–Jacobi–Bellman equations (Equation 46) after and before tipping become

$$\rho V_a(s) = \max_y \Big[U(y) + V_a'(s)\Big(G_a(s) - y\Big)\Big],$$

$$\rho V_b(s) = \max_y \Big[U(y) - h\Big(V_b(s) - V_a(s)\Big) + V_b'(s)\Big(G_b(s) - y\Big)\Big]. \tag{53}$$

Before tipping, the second equation of Equation 53 applies. The optimality condition becomes

$$U'(y) = V_b'(s). \tag{54}$$

By differentiating the second equation of Equation 53 with respect to s, and using the optimality condition (Equation 54) for $y(s)$, the terms $U'(y)y'$ and $-V_b'(s)y'$ cancel out (envelope theorem), so that

$$V_b''(s)\Big(G_b(s) - y(s)\Big) = \Big(\rho - G_b'(s) + h\Big)V_b'(s) - hV_a'(s). \tag{55}$$

For the *CRRA* utility function $U(y) = y^{1-\sigma}/(1 - \sigma)$, with $U'(y) = y^{-\sigma}$ and $U''(s) = -\sigma y^{-\sigma-1}$, using the optimality condition (Equation 54) again, Equation 55 becomes the differential equation in y

$$\Big(G_b(s) - y(s)\Big)y'(s) = \sigma^{-1}\Big[G_b'(s) - \rho - h\Big(1 - V_a'(s)/y^{-\sigma}(s)\Big)\Big]y(s). \tag{56}$$

Using the differential equation in Equation 52, differential Equation 56 becomes in the time domain

$$\dot{y}(t) = \sigma^{-1}\Big[G_b'\Big(s(t)\Big) - \rho - h\Big(1 - V_a'\Big(s(t)\Big)/y^{-\sigma}(t)\Big)\Big]y(t). \tag{57}$$

The stable manifold of the dynamical system consisting of the differential equations in Equations 52 and 57 towards the steady state of this dynamical system yields the same curve as the stable solution of the differential Equation 56.

After tipping, the first equation of Equation 53 applies. The solution follows immediately from the solution before tipping by setting the hazard rate $h = 0$.

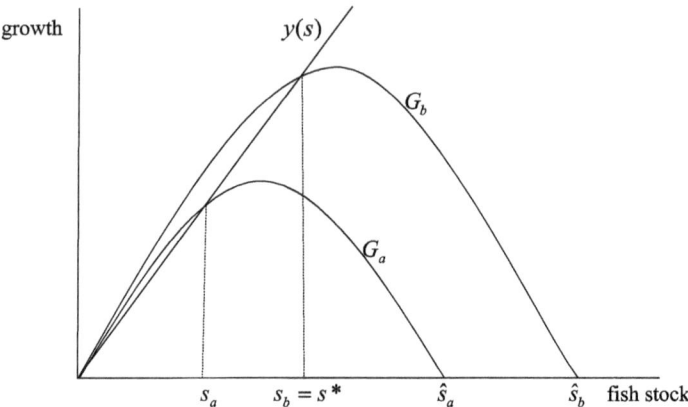

Figure 8 Linear harvesting policies.

The optimality condition becomes $U'(y) = V_a'(s)$, and the differential equations in y (in the state domain and in the time domain) become

$$\left(G_a(s) - y(s)\right)y'(s) = \sigma^{-1}\left(G_a'(s) - \rho\right)y(s),$$
$$\dot{y}(t) = \sigma^{-1}\left(G_a'(s(t)) - \rho\right)y(t).$$

(58)

Note that the logistic growth function $G(s) = gs(1 - s/\hat{s})$ has $G'(s) = g(1 - 2s/\hat{s})$. It follows that for $\sigma^{-1} = 0.5$, the first differential equation of Equation 58 has the linear solution $y_a(s) = 0.5(\rho + g)s$. This is the optimal harvesting policy after tipping. It is also the optimal harvesting policy in the absence of tipping, and it is the optimal harvesting policy before tipping because $y_b(s) = 0.5(\rho + g)s$ solves the differential Equation 56. The third term between square brackets in Equation 56 becomes 0, because $V_a'(s) = U'\left(y_a(s)\right) = \left(y_a(s)\right)^{-\sigma}$. Figure 8 shows the situation for $\sigma^{-1} = 0.5$.

The conclusion is that if the elasticity of intertemporal substitution $\sigma^{-1} = 0.5$, basically the same story results as in Section 4.2. Before tipping, the fishery behaves as if there is no risk of tipping, and the optimal path follows the linear stable manifold $y(s) = 0.5(\rho + g)s$ up to the steady state s_b given by the golden rule $G_b'(s_b) = G_b'(s^*) = \rho$. At the tipping point, the fishery adjusts. If the fish stock s has passed s_a, the optimal path follows the stable manifold back to the steady state s_a given by the golden rule $G_a'(s_a) = \rho$. The difference with Section 4.2 is that the optimal path up to s_b is not a moratorium and the optimal path back to s_a is not instantaneous.

The story changes if the elasticity of intertemporal substitution $\sigma^{-1} \neq 0.5$. In this case, it is difficult to solve the first differential equation of Equation 58 for the optimal harvesting policy $y_a(s)$ after tipping. However, it is possible to characterize precaution in this fishery by looking at the slope of $y_a(s)$ in the steady state $\left(s_a, G_a(s_a)\right)$. Using the first equation of Equation 58 for $y_a'(s)$, l'Hôpital's rule yields a quadratic equation for the slope $y_a'(s_a)$ of $y_a(s)$ in the steady state:

$$
y_a'(s_a) = \lim_{s \to s_a} \frac{\sigma^{-1}\left(G_a'(s) - \rho\right)y_a'(s) + \sigma^{-1}G_a''(s)y_a(s)}{G_a'(s) - y_a'(s)} \Rightarrow
$$

$$
y_a'(s_a)\left(\rho - y_a'(s_a)\right) = \sigma^{-1}G_a''(s_a)G_a(s_a). \tag{59}
$$

The phase diagram in the time domain implies that the slope $y_a'(s_a)$ in the steady state $\left(s_a, G_a(s_a)\right)$ is the positive root of the quadratic equation Equation 59, that is,

$$
y_a'(s_a) = 0.5\left(\rho + \sqrt{\rho^2 - 4\sigma^{-1}G_a''(s_a)G_a(s_a)}\right). \tag{60}
$$

Because $G''(s) = 2g/\hat{s}$, $2G''(s)G(s) = \left(G'(s)\right)^2 - g^2$, and $G_a'(s_a) = \rho$, this becomes

$$
y_a'(s_a) = 0.5\left(\rho + \sqrt{\rho^2 - 2\sigma^{-1}(\rho^2 - g^2)}\right). \tag{61}
$$

If the elasticity of intertemporal substitution $\sigma^{-1} = 0.5$, the slope $y_a'(s_a) = 0.5(\rho + g)$, confirming the previous analysis. However, if $\sigma^{-1} < 0.5$, the slope $y_a'(s_a)$ is smaller than $0.5(\rho + g)$, so that the stable manifold $y_a(s)$ bends away below the line $0.5(\rho + g)s$. The stable manifold $y_a(s)$ passes below the steady state $\left(s^*, G_b(s^*)\right)$, so that harvesting y jumps down to this stable manifold when tipping occurs in that steady state. The steady-state fish stock s_b before tipping cannot be equal to s^*, because s^* does not solve the golden rule

$$
G_b'(s_b) = \rho + h\left(1 - y_a^{-\sigma}(s_b)/G_b^{-\sigma}(s_b)\right), \tag{62}
$$

which follows from Equation 56 with $V_a'(s_b) = \left(y_a(s_b)\right)^{-\sigma}$ and $y_b(s_b) = G_b(s_b)$. The second term on the right-hand side of Equation 62 is not equal to 0 for $s_b = s^*$. This term must be negative, because harvesting y jumps down from $G_b(s_b)$ to $y_a(s_b)$ if tipping occurs in the steady state s_b. It follows that $G_b'(s_b) < \rho$, and thus $s_b > s^*$. In fact, s_b lies between s^* and the intersection point of the stable manifold $y_a(s)$ and the growth curve $G_b(s)$.

Figure 9 shows the situation and labels the s_b that results for $\sigma^{-1} < 0.5$ as s_{b2} (the stable manifold is depicted as a line but note that it is not linear). This means

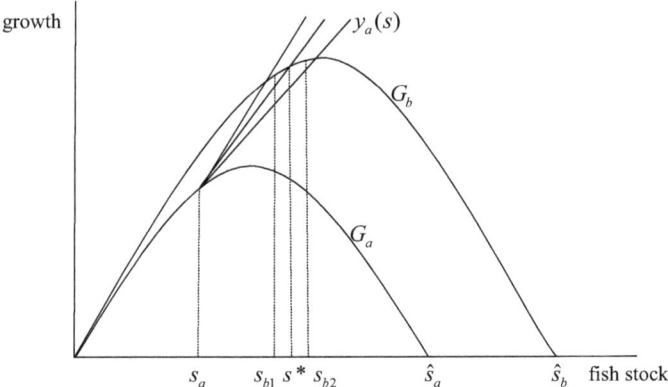

Figure 9 Intertemporal substitution elasticity in fishery.

that harvesting becomes precautionary because it aims for a higher steady-state fish stock than in the absence of tipping. If the hazard rate h increases, the steady-state fish stock s_{b2} moves closer to the intersection point, so that precaution increases. Similarly, if the elasticity of intertemporal substitution $\sigma^{-1} > 0.5$, the slope $y_a{'}(s_a)$ is larger than $0.5(\rho + g)$, so that the stable manifold $y_a(s)$ bends away above the line $0.5(\rho + g)s$. The second term on the right-hand side of Equation 62 must be positive, because harvesting y jumps up from $G_b(s_b)$ to $y_a(s_b)$ if tipping occurs in the steady state s_b. It follows that $G_b{'}(s_b) > \rho$ and $s_b < s^*$. Again, s_b lies between s^* and the intersection point of the stable manifold $y_a(s)$ and the growth curve $G_b(s)$, but now to the left of s^*. Figure 9 shows this situation as well and labels the s_b that results for $\sigma^{-1} > 0.5$ as s_{b1}. This means that harvesting now increases the exploitation because it aims for a lower steady-state fish stock than in the absence of tipping. If the hazard rate h increases, the steady-state fish stock s_{b1} moves closer to the other intersection point, so that the exploitation increases further. The previous analysis yields the following proposition.

Proposition 1: For the targeted steady-state fish stock before tipping s_b, $s_b > s^*$, if $\sigma^{-1} < 0.5$, and $s_b < s^*$, if $\sigma^{-1} > 0.5$, where s^* is the steady-state fish stock in the absence of tipping. This means that optimal harvesting is precautionary, if the elasticity of intertemporal substitution is below 0.5, and increases exploitation, if the elasticity of intertemporal substitution is above 0.5.

The basic argument is a smoothing argument. If the optimal path $y_a(s)$ toward the steady state after tipping is less steep, the targeted steady-state fish stock before tipping s_b is higher, to reduce the jump down in harvesting at the tipping point. However, if the optimal path $y_a(s)$ toward the steady state after tipping is steeper, the opposite pattern occurs. Furthermore, a low elasticity of intertemporal substitution means that the slope of the optimal path $y_a(s)$ is less steep, but a high elasticity of intertemporal substitution has the opposite effect.

A numerical example helps to get the picture. Using $G'(s) = g(1 - 2s/\hat{s})$, it follows that $s^* = 30$ and $s_a = 24$, if $g = 0.05, \rho = 0.02, \hat{s}_b = 100$, and $\hat{s}_a = 80$. For $h = 0.05$, it follows from Equation 62, by calculating the stable manifolds $y_a(s)$ numerically, that $s_{b1} = 28.65$ if $\sigma^{-1} = 1 > 0.5$ and $s_{b2} = 31.53$ if $\sigma^{-1} = 0.33 < 0.5$.

The purpose of this section was to show that precaution or increased exploitation can result for a constant or exogenous hazard rate in case of a more general utility of harvest. Of course, the result from Section 4.2 that an endogenous hazard rate leads to precaution still stands. It follows that for an endogenous hazard rate and a more general utility of harvest, precaution is either enhanced or reduced or turned into increased exploitation (see for an example de Zeeuw and He, 2017).

4.4 Concluding Remarks

Section 4.2 shows that the standard linear fishery with a fixed price has the stylized result that the risk of tipping does not lead to a change in behavior when the hazard rate is exogenous but leads to precaution when the hazard rate is endogenous. This result follows from the possibility that the fishery can immediately adjust to a new steady-state fish stock when tipping occurs. Section 4.3 shows that for an extension to a general utility of harvest, where the price is not fixed, or when the model is used for a general environmental economics problem with logistic growth and a limited carrying capacity, the risk of tipping has two effects. The hazard rate itself can lead to precaution or increased exploitation, depending on the elasticity of intertemporal substitution. Endogeneity of the hazard rate has a precautionary effect, because a higher fish stock decreases the hazard rate. The results follow from the golden rule for the fishery before tipping, which determines the steady-state fish stock before tipping. The Hamilton–Jacobi–Bellman equation before tipping (the second equation of Equation 58 with hazard rate $h(s)$) leads to the golden rule. The risk of tipping into a regime with the lower current value $V_a < V_b$ is reflected in the term $h(s)\big(V_b(s) - V_a(s)\big)$. Differentiation of this term with respect to s yields besides $h(s)\big(V_b'(s) - V_a'(s)\big)$ also $h'(s)\big(V_b(s) - V_a(s)\big)$. Following the same steps as in Equations 54, 55, and 56, but keeping $V_b'(s)$, leads to the golden rule

$$G_b'(s_b) = \rho + h(s_b)\left(1 - \frac{V_a'(s_b)}{V_b'(s_b)}\right) + h'(s_b)\left(\frac{V_b(s_b) - V_a(s_b)}{V_b'(s_b)}\right). \tag{63}$$

The third term on the right-hand side of Equation 63 is negative, so that the steady-state fish stock is pushed up. The second term on the right-hand side of Equation 63 is 0 for the linear fishery in Section 4.2, so that behavior becomes precautionary. However, it can be positive or negative in Section 4.3, so that precaution is either enhanced or reduced or turned into increased exploitation. It depends on the parameters of the fishery what the overall result will be.

4.5 Ramsey Growth and Climate Tipping

The Introduction describes that in the history of economics and the environment, concern shifted from the availability of certain resources to the protection of ecosystems that provide a wide variety of resources and services. A good example is the shift from concern about the availability of fossil fuels to concern about the accumulation of CO_2 and climate change by burning these fossil fuels. Integrating the threat of climate change into economic analysis has become widespread now, and this research got recognition when in 2018, the Prize in Economics in honour of Alfred Nobel was awarded to William Nordhaus for developing the DICE (Dynamic Integrated Climate-Economy) model (Nordhaus, 2008). The crucial mechanism in the DICE model is the rise in the temperature (by accumulating greenhouse gases in the atmosphere) that affects the total factor productivity of the economy. The model is a Ramsey growth model with a feedback mechanism that connects the emissions of greenhouse gases from using fossil fuels in the economy via a temperature rise to a lower total factor productivity. Climatologists predict that the climate probably has tipping points, as described in the Introduction (Lenton et al., 2008). It is uncertain when these tipping points will occur, and what the precise effect will be. However, climate tipping can be modelled with a hazard rate and a possible shock to the total factor productivity, with a sensitivity analysis on the size of the shock. The analysis of the Ramsey growth model with climate tipping is partly the same as the analysis of a fishery in Section 4.3 but partly also different. Climate tipping implies a shock to a parameter (total factor productivity) in the dynamical equation for the accumulation of capital k. However, an endogenous hazard rate depends on the stock of greenhouse gases p, and not on the capital stock k. For an exogenous hazard rate h, the analysis leading to the targeted capital stock before tipping is the same as in the Section 4.3 for the targeted fish stock before tipping. However, an endogenous hazard rate is related to the emissions of greenhouse gases. This means that these emissions have a cost on top of the regular *social cost of carbon*, which is the gradual damage to the total factor productivity from carbon emissions. Implementing the optimal path in the Ramsey growth model with climate tipping requires levying a tax on the greenhouse gas emissions equal to the *total* social cost of carbon. This tax reduces emissions by substituting the use of fossil fuels either with the use of renewables or with an investment in a larger capital stock. The analysis starts with an exogenous hazard rate, so that the accumulation of greenhouse gases does not play a role in climate tipping. An endogenous hazard rate requires an analysis with two stock variables, one for the capital stock and one for the stock of greenhouse gases. The risk of climate tipping leads to a targeted level of the capital stock before tipping, as in the fishery, but also to an increase in the tax on emissions of greenhouse gases to reduce the stock of greenhouse gases and the probability of climate tipping.

In a simple Ramsey growth model, production is allocated over consumption c and investment in capital k to maximize intertemporal utility U of consumption c. Welfare maximization becomes

$$\max_{c(.)} \int_0^\infty e^{-\rho t} U\Big(c(t)\Big) dt,$$

$$\dot{k}(t) = F\Big(k(t)\Big) - c(t), k(0) = k_0, \tag{64}$$

where $F(k)$ denotes the net production function, ρ the discount rate, and k_0 the initial stock.

The consequences of climate tipping are modelled as a shock to the total factor productivity. This results from a structural change in the climate system. In terms of the so-called climate sensitivity, which indicates the warming when the amount of greenhouse gases in the atmosphere doubles, the climate sensitivity jumps, for example, from 3 to 4 degrees when tipping occurs. This implies a drop in the total factor productivity. The production function $F_b(k) = \alpha\sqrt{k}$, for example, shifts to $F_a(k) = \beta\alpha\sqrt{k}, 0 < \beta < 1$, where α denotes the total factor productivity.

For an exogenous hazard rate h, the analysis is the same as for the fishery in the Section 4.3. The golden rules of capital accumulation are $F_a'(k_a) = \rho$ after tipping and $F_b'(k^*) = \rho$ in the absence of tipping, while before tipping, the golden rule becomes (see Equation 62)

$$F_b'(k_b) = \rho + h\Big(1 - c_a^{-\sigma}(k_b)/F_b^{-\sigma}(k_b)\Big), \tag{65}$$

where $c_a(k)$ is the stable manifold or the optimal path of consumption after tipping, and k_a, k^*, and k_b denote the respective steady-state capital stocks.

The stable manifold $c_a(k)$ is the solution of the differential equation (see Equation 58)

$$\left(F_a(k) - c_a(k)\right)c_a{}'(k) = \sigma^{-1}\left(F_a{}'(k) - \rho\right)c_a(k). \tag{66}$$

In the steady state $(k_a, F_a(k_a))$ after tipping, the slope of this stable manifold is

$$c_a{}'(k_a) = 0.5\left(\rho + \sqrt{\rho^2 - 4\sigma^{-1}F_a{}''(k_a)F_a(k_a)}\right). \tag{67}$$

Because $F'(k) = 0.5ak^{-0.5}$, $F''(k) = -0.25ak^{-1.5}$, $F''(k)F(k) = -\left(F'(k)\right)^2$, and $F_a{}'(k_a) = \rho$,

$$c_a{}'(k_a) = 0.5\left(\rho + \sqrt{\rho^2 + 4\sigma^{-1}\rho^2}\right). \tag{68}$$

If the elasticity of intertemporal substitution $\sigma^{-1} = 2$, the slope $c_a{}'(k_a) = 2\rho$, and the linear stable manifold $c_a(k) = 2\rho k$ is the solution of the differential Equation 66. This is the optimal path of consumption after tipping, but also the optimal path of consumption in the absence of tipping and before tipping. The economy before tipping targets for the same capital stock as in the absence of tipping. The only difference with the analysis of the fishery in Section 4.3 is that this linear path of reference follows for the elasticity of substitution $\sigma^{-1} = 2$, and not for $\sigma^{-1} = 0.5$. The reason is that the functional forms of the production function F and the growth function G for the fishery differ. The rest of the analysis is the same as in Section 4.3.

Figure 10 looks like Figure 9. If $\sigma^{-1} < 2$, the stable manifold $c_a(k)$ passes below the steady state $\left(k^*, F_b(k^*)\right)$. The targeted capital stock k_b is larger than k^*, implying precautionary saving. If $\sigma^{-1} > 2$, the stable manifold $c_a(k)$ passes

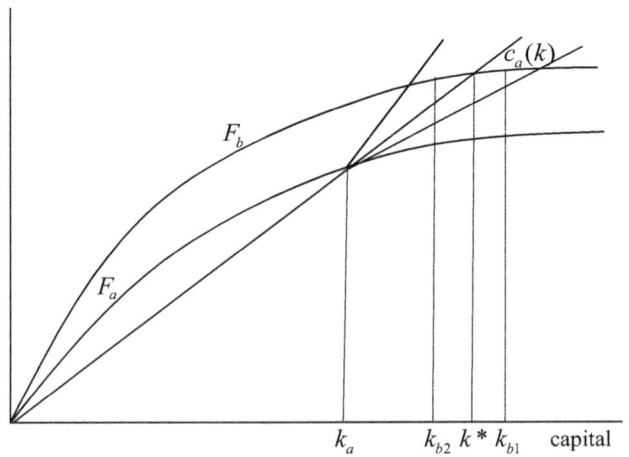

Figure 10 Intertemporal substitution elasticity in Ramsey growth.

above the steady state $\left(k^*, F_b(k^*)\right)$. The targeted capital stock k_b is smaller than k^*, which implies less saving than in the absence of tipping. These results depend, of course, on the specific functional form of the production function, that is, $F(k) = a\sqrt{k}$. However, for an increasing concave production function F, the slope of the stable manifold $c_a(k)$ increases for an increasing elasticity of intertemporal substitution σ^{-1}. A separating value of σ^{-1} exists for which the stable manifold $c_a(k)$ intersects the production function F_b in the steady state $\left(k^*, F_b\left(k^*\right)\right)$. The conclusion of Section 4.3 remains but for a different value of σ^{-1}.

Proposition 2: For the targeted steady-state capital stock before tipping k_b, it holds that $k_b > k^*$ if σ^{-1} is small, and $k_b < k^*$ if σ^{-1} is big, where k^* is the steady-state capital stock in the absence of tipping. This implies that the optimal saving is precautionary, if the elasticity of intertemporal substitution is low, but the optimal saving is lower than in the absence of tipping if the elasticity of intertemporal substitution is high.

The elasticity of intertemporal substitution can be interpreted as the inverse of intergenerational inequality aversion. This implies that the optimal saving is precautionary if this inequality aversion is high. It follows that the prospect of possible climate tipping requires one to save more and consume less if the intergenerational inequality aversion is sufficiently high.

For an endogenous hazard rate $h(p)$, the analysis differs from the analysis of the fishery in Section 4.3. The hazard rate of climate tipping depends on the stock of greenhouse gases p, and not on the capital stock k. Emissions of greenhouse gases e result from the use of fossil fuels (also denoted by e for a proper choice of dimensions) as an input factor into the production function $\widetilde{F}(k, e)$. The emissions e accumulate into a stock of greenhouse gases s according to

$$\dot{p}(t) = e(t) - \delta p(t), p(0) = p_0, \tag{69}$$

where δ denotes the natural assimilation rate and p_0 the initial stock of greenhouse gases.

The fossil fuels are available at a price π. For each level of the capital stock k, maximization of $\widetilde{F}_a(k, e) - \pi e$ over e yields the optimal use of fossil fuels and the net production function $F_a(k)$. After tipping, the problem is the same as for the exogenous hazard rate h above but before tipping, the Hamilton–Jacobi–Bellman equation becomes

$$pV_b(k, p) = \max_{c,e} \left[U(c) - h(p)\left(V_b(k, p) - V_a(k)\right) + \right.$$
$$\left. V_{bk}(k, p)\left(\widetilde{F}_b(k, e) - \pi e - c\right) + V_{bp}(k, p)(e - \delta p) \right], \tag{70}$$

where V_b denotes the current value function before tipping. Note that V_b has two state variables, k and p, but V_a only one, because the accumulation of greenhouse gases does not matter anymore after climate tipping. The optimality conditions become

$$U'(c) = V_{bk}(k,p), \tilde{F}_{be}(k,e) = \pi - V_{bp}(k,p)/V_{bk}(k,p). \tag{71}$$

The term $-V_{bp}(k,p)/V_{bk}(k,p)$ in the second condition of Equation 71 can be interpreted as the additional social cost of carbon. A carbon tax τ equal to this term corrects for this externality. It pushes down the stream of greenhouse gas emissions e and thus the stock of greenhouse gases p and the hazard rate $h(p)$. Levying this tax τ, the optimal use of fossil fuels e yields the net production function $\hat{F}_b(k,\tau)$, which depends on the tax τ now. By substituting the optimal consumption c and use of fossil fuels e from Equation 71 into Equation 70, and then by partially differentiating Equation 70 with respect to k and to p, some terms cancel out using Equation 71 (envelope theorem). Finally, this procedure yields in the time domain (omitting the time dependence of k, p, and τ)

$$\begin{aligned}
\dot{V}_{bk}(k,p) &= \left(\rho + h(p) - \hat{F}_{bk}(k,\tau)\right)V_{bk}(k,p) - h(p)V_a'(k), \\
\dot{V}_{bp}(k,p) &= \left(\rho + \delta + h(p)\right)V_{bp}(k,p) + h'(p)\left(V_b(k,p) - V_a(k)\right),
\end{aligned} \tag{72}$$

assuming that $V_{bpk} = V_{bkp}$, where $\dot{V}_{bk} = V_{bkk}\dot{k} + V_{bkp}\dot{p}$ and $\dot{V}_{bp} = V_{bpk}\dot{k} + V_{bpp}\dot{p}$. The first condition of Equation 71 yields $V_{bk} = U'(c) = c^{-\sigma}$ and $\dot{V}_{bk} = U''(c)\dot{c} = -\sigma U'(c)\dot{c}/c$, and the first equation of Equation 72 leads to the Keynes–Ramsey rule before climate tipping (see also Equation 57)

$$\dot{c}(t) = \sigma^{-1}\left[\hat{F}_{bk}\left(k(t),\tau(t)\right) - \rho - h\left(p(t)\right)\left(1 - V_a'\left(k(t)\right)/c^{-\sigma}(t)\right)\right]c(t). \tag{73}$$

The path of the carbon tax $\tau(t)$ affects the path of the net production $\hat{F}_b\left(k(t),\tau(t)\right)$ and determines the path of greenhouse gas emissions $e(t)$, and thus the path of the stock of greenhouse gases $p(t)$ according to Equation 69. Furthermore, $\dot{\tau}/\tau = \dot{V}_{bp}(k,p)/V_{bp}(k,p) - \dot{V}_{bk}(k,p)/V_{bk}(k,p)$ holds, because $\tau = -V_{bp}(k,p)/V_{bk}(k,p)$, so that the two equations of Equation 72 yield

$$\begin{aligned}
\dot{\tau}(t) = &[\hat{F}_{bk}\left(k(t),\tau(t)\right) + \delta + h\left(p(t)\right)\left(V_a'\left(k(t)\right)/c^{-\sigma}(t)\right)]\tau(t) \\
&-h'\left(p(t)\right)\left(\left(V_b\left(k(t),p(t)\right) - V_a\left(k(t)\right)\right)/c^{-\sigma}(t)\right).
\end{aligned} \tag{74}$$

The purpose of the carbon tax τ is to regulate the use of fossil fuels e, and not to raise revenues. The proceeds τe are returned to the economy. Note that $e = -\hat{F}_{b\tau}(k, \tau)$. It follows that the solution before climate tipping is a four-dimensional dynamical system consisting of the Keynes–Ramsey rule (Equation 73), the carbon tax rule (Equation 74), the accumulation of capital

$$\dot{k}(t) = \hat{F}_b\Big(k(t), \tau(t)\Big) - \tau(t)\hat{F}_{b\tau}\Big(k(t), \tau(t)\Big) - c(t), k(0) = k_0, \tag{75}$$

and the accumulation of greenhouse gases

$$\dot{p}(t) = -\hat{F}_{b\tau}\Big(k(t), \tau(t)\Big) - \delta p(t), p(0) = p_0. \tag{76}$$

This dynamical system is complicated, but it has a familiar structure. It has two state variables (k and p) with initial conditions and two co-state variables (c and τ). Under the usual assumptions, the optimal path will jump to the stable manifold and converge to the steady state. This is a *target* steady state before climate tipping because at the tipping point, the optimal path will jump to the stable manifold and converge to the steady state after climate tipping, so that the target steady state will not be reached. The target steady state k_b is the solution of the golden rule that follows from setting the terms between brackets in the Keynes–Ramsey rule (Equation 73) equal to 0 (see also Equation 65). The steady-state tax τ_b lowers the use of fossil fuel e. This has two effects. First, it lowers the steady-state stock of greenhouse gases p_b and thus the hazard rate $h(p_b)$, which implies that if savings are precautionary, this result is mitigated. Second, it affects the level of production $\hat{F}_b$ in the steady state, and thus also affects whether precautionary saving results or not, because the level of production determines whether consumption jumps down or not when climate tipping occurs.

Reducing the risk of climate tipping induces a carbon tax on top of the carbon tax that corrects the regular social cost of carbon, which is the gradual damage to the total factor productivity from the carbon emissions. When modelling the gradual damage to the total factor productivity in the production functions before and after tipping, that is, $F_b(k) = \alpha\sqrt{k}$ and $F_a(k) = \beta\alpha\sqrt{k}$, $0 < \beta < 1$, the total factor productivity α depends on the stock of greenhouse gases p, with marginal damages $\alpha'(p)$. Marginal damages become $\alpha'(p) = -\eta\alpha(p)$, with damage parameter η, when damages are approximated by exponential decay (Golosov et al., 2014). In the previous analysis, this implies that the accumulation of greenhouse gases also plays a role after climate tipping (so that a carbon tax is needed there as well), and an additional role before climate tipping.

The current value function after climate tipping V_a now has two state variables, k and p, and it is the solution of the Hamilton–Jacobi–Bellman equation

$$\rho V_a(k,p) = \max_{c,e}[U(c) + V_{ak}(k,p)\left(\widetilde{F}_a(k,p,e) - \pi e - c\right)$$
$$+V_{ap}(k,p)(e - \delta p)], \tag{77}$$

where the production function now also depends on p.

Equation 77 had the same structure as Equation 70 for $h = 0$, and the analysis leads to

$$\dot{V}_{ak}(k,p) = \left(\rho - \hat{F}_{ak}(k,p,\tau)\right)V_{ak}(k,p),$$
$$\dot{V}_{ap}(k,p) = (\rho + \delta)V_{ap}(k,p) + \eta V_{ak}(k,p)\hat{F}_a(k,p,\tau). \tag{78}$$

The first equation of Equation 78 yields the Keynes–Ramsey rule after climate tipping, and both equations of Equation 78 yield for the carbon tax $\tau = -V_{ap}(k,p)/V_{ak}(k,p)$ after climate tipping

$$\dot{\tau}(t) = [\hat{F}_{ak}\left(k(t),p(t),\tau(t)\right) + \delta]\tau(t) - \eta\hat{F}_a\left(k(t),p(t),\tau(t)\right). \tag{79}$$

In steady state, $\dot{\tau} = 0$ and $\hat{F}_{ak} = \rho$, so that the steady-state carbon tax τ_a is equal to the marginal damage discounted by the discount rate ρ plus the natural assimilation rate δ.

The current value function before climate tipping V_b is still the solution of the Hamilton–Jacobi–Bellman equation (Equation 70), but the current value function after climate tipping V_a now depends on k and p, and $\widetilde{F}$ depends on p via the total factor productivity $\alpha(p)$, $\alpha'(p) = -\eta\alpha(p)$. It follows that the second equation of Equation 72 has two extra terms, $\eta V_{bk}(k,p)\hat{F}(k,p,\tau)$ and $-h(p)V_{ap}(k,p)$, so that the equation for the total carbon tax τ before tipping changes into

$$\dot{\tau}(t) = [\hat{F}_{bk}\left(k(t),p(t),\tau(t)\right) + \delta + h\left(p(t)\right)\left(V_{ak}\left(k(t),p(t)\right)/c^{-\gamma}(t)\right)]\tau(t)$$
$$-\eta\hat{F}_b\left(k(t),p(t),\tau(t)\right) + h\left(p(t)\right)\left(V_{ap}\left(k(t),p(t)\right)/c^{-\gamma}(t)\right)$$
$$-h'\left(p(t)\right)\left(\left(V_b\left(k(t),p(t)\right) - V_a\left(k(t),p(t)\right)\right)\right)/c^{-\gamma}(t). \tag{80}$$

Equation 80 is complicated, but note that for $h = 0$, the steady-state carbon tax τ_b is again equal to the marginal damage discounted by the discount rate ρ plus the natural assimilation rate δ. If climate tipping can occur, so that the hazard rate h is not equal to 0, discounting changes and the carbon tax τ has two additional components. One additional component follows from the last term on the right-hand side of Equation 80. This is the same as the last term on the right-hand side of Equation 74, where marginal damages are ignored, and it corrects for the risk of climate tipping. The other additional component follows from the term before the last one on the right-hand side of Equation 80. It corrects for the risk of lowering the current value V_a after climate tipping for an increasing stock of greenhouse gases p. This tax component lowers the stakes of tipping. The carbon tax before tipping thus has three components: a conventional one, one that reduces the risk of tipping, and one that lowers the stakes. It is interesting to see in the presentation of a calibration below how big these different components of the carbon tax before tipping are.

It is time to take stock of where the analysis stands. The analysis of a Ramsey growth model with climate tipping splits into a dynamical optimization problem after tipping and one before tipping. If the accumulation of greenhouse gases only affects the hazard rate of climate tipping as a shock to the total factor productivity, and not the gradual damage, the problem after tipping is a standard Ramsey growth model, with only a Keynes–Ramsey rule for optimal consumption. If there is also gradual damage to the total factor productivity, the solution after tipping also yields a rule for the carbon tax to correct for the marginal damages. If the hazard rate is exogenous, only a carbon tax is needed to correct for the marginal damages, both before and after climate tipping. However, if the hazard rate is endogenous and depends on the stock of greenhouse gases, an additional carbon tax is needed to correct for the risk of climate tipping. This carbon tax must also take account of the effect of a larger stock of greenhouse gases on the value after climate tipping.

The model can be easily extended further by adding the option of using renewables in production at a fixed price, which gives the additional option of substituting the use of fossil fuels. Solving the problem after climate tipping yields the current value function after tipping. Before climate tipping, a four-dimensional dynamical system results, consisting of a Keynes–Ramsey rule, a carbon tax rule, the accumulation of capital, and the accumulation of greenhouse gases. A numerical analysis is needed to get more insight. The Cobb–Douglas production function allows for the substitution possibilities. Data sources are the BP Statistical Review and the World Bank Development Indicators in 2010. Furthermore, the discount rate $\rho = 0.014$, the elasticity of intertemporal substitution $\sigma^{-1} = 0.5$ (or 0.8 in a sensitivity test), the shock to the total factor productivity $\beta = 0.8$ (or 0.9 in a sensitivity test), the natural assimilation rate $\delta = 0.003$ (with an effective emission rate of 0.5), and the marginal damage parameter $\eta = 0.02379$. The hazard rate $h(p)$ has a base value 0.025, and increases linearly with p. All details of this calibration are available

Table 1 Steady-states Ramsey growth with climate tipping.

	No tipping	20% shock total factor productivity		10% shock total factor productivity	
		After tipping	Target before	After tipping	Target before
Capital stock (trillion $)	378	271	492	323	431
Consumption (trillion $)	57.1	40.8	58.3	48.7	57.8
Carbon stock (gigatons)	1502	1107	1287	1303	1425
Temperature (°C)	4.00	2.68	3.33	3.38	3.77
Precaution (%/year)	0	0	1.10	0	0.57
Carbon tax ($/ton of CO_2)	15.4	11.0	54.8	13.2	29.8
Marginal damage	15.4	11.0	4.3	13.2	3.8
Averting risk	0	0	35.0	0	12.4
Lowering stakes	0	0	15.4	0	13.7

in van der Ploeg and de Zeeuw (2019). Table 1 provides the results for the targeted steady state.

Precaution can be positive or negative depending on whether the targeted capital stock is higher or lower than in the absence of climate tipping. Apparently, for the reasonable value of the elasticity of intertemporal substitution $\sigma^{-1} = 0.5$, the value of this term is positive, implying that the optimal saving is precautionary. A sensitivity analysis with the elasticity of intertemporal substitution $\sigma^{-1} = 0.8$ affects the targeted capital stock but saving remains precautionary, although saving is lower. The carbon tax and the other variables are hardly affected.

The steady-state capital stocks k_a after tipping are lower than the steady-state capital stock k^* in the absence of climate tipping because of the shocks to the total factor productivity. The targeted steady-state capital stocks k_b before climate tipping are substantially higher than in the absence of climate tipping, with precautionary saving. The target increases for an increasing expected drop in the total factor productivity. The target steady-state stock of greenhouse gases p_b before climate tipping decreases for an increasing expected drop in the total factor productivity. The consumption jumps down and moves to the lower steady-state level c_a after climate tipping.

Table 1 shows the decomposition of the target steady-state carbon tax τ_b before climate tipping. First note that the steady-state carbon tax $\tau^* = 15.4$ $ per ton of CO_2 that results in the absence of climate tipping (which only corrects for the marginal damages) is close to $12 per ton of CO_2 in the analysis with the DICE model (Nordhaus, 2014). When climate tipping can occur, the value of the target steady-state carbon tax τ_b before tipping substantially increases to $29.8 per ton of CO_2 for an expected drop in the total factor productivity of 10%, and to $54.8 per ton of CO_2 for an expected drop of 20%. The decomposition shows that the component that corrects for the marginal damages is low but the component that corrects for the risk of climate tipping is high, especially for a high expected drop in the total factor productivity.

4.6 Extensions

Three extensions of the analysis in Section 4.5 deserve some attention. First, the tipping point is well-defined in the sense that the climate system shifts to another domain of attraction, but it does not mean that the full shock to the total factor productivity materializes immediately (van der Ploeg and de Zeeuw, 2018). This impact delay affects the savings response. If a potential climate tipping point induces more saving and thus targets for a higher capital stock, a sufficiently large delay in the impact of the shock may turn this effect around and induce less saving, and thus targets for a lower capital stock than in case the risk of climate tipping is ignored.

Second, the analysis in Section 4.5 maximizes expected utility in which the parameter σ indicates both the relative risk aversion and the intergenerational inequality aversion (or the inverse of the elasticity of intertemporal substitution). However, by using Kreps–Porteus (1978) or Epstein–Zin (1989) preferences, it is possible to separate these two aspects of preferences. Cai et al. (2012) use Epstein–Zin preferences in their analysis of an extension of the DICE model where climate tipping induces an upward shift in the damage function. They find a substantial increase in the carbon tax, but they do not compare this with the outcome under expected utility. Lemoine and Traeger (2016) use these preferences in a discrete-time analysis of climate tipping. They conclude that it does not change optimal policy very much. Epstein–Zin preferences can be incorporated into the Hamilton–Jacobi–Bellman framework (Duffie and Epstein, 1992) and van der Ploeg and de Zeeuw (2018) apply this technique to the Ramsey growth model with climate tipping given in Section 4.5. They do not find large changes in optimal policy either but for the empirically relevant case of a greater dislike for risk than for intertemporal fluctuations, the savings response is stronger.

Third, climate change is a global environmental problem, and an optimal climate policy requires voluntary cooperation between sovereign states.

Furthermore, the developed states in the "North" usually have a higher initial capital stock and are less vulnerable to climate catastrophes than the states in the "South." In the absence of cooperation, so that transboundary externalities are ignored, a Nash equilibrium for the climate policies of the North and the South characterizes the outcome. The model in Section 4.5 changes into two models of the same type but with a higher initial capital stock in the North and a higher shock to the total factor productivity in the South. The models are connected, because the emissions of greenhouse gases from both regions accumulate into the stock of greenhouse gases in Equation 69. When the North and the South cooperate, they maximize the sum of their welfare indicators, and the problem is basically the same as in Section 4.5. When the two regions do not cooperate, each region maximizes its own welfare indicator, given the path of greenhouse gas emissions in the other region. In this case, the current value functions also become a function of time, but the analysis remains essentially the same. For an initial capital stock in the North, which is nine times larger than the initial capital stock in the South, and for a shock of 10% to the total factor productivity in the North and 30% in the South, the conclusions are as follows (van der Ploeg and de Zeeuw, 2016). The carbon taxes are lower in the absence of cooperation, as is to be expected, so that the risk of tipping is higher, and the savings response is stronger. If the North and the South cooperate, they target for a high common carbon tax, but initially they allow for a lower carbon tax in the South, so that the South can catch up. If the regions do not cooperate, the North always has a low carbon tax. The South starts with a low carbon tax (priority to growth) but later has a high carbon tax (priority to reducing the risk of climate tipping).

4.7 Concluding Remarks

Section 4.5 shows that the Ramsey growth model with climate tipping has the stylized result that the risk of climate tipping leads to precautionary saving or less saving (depending on the elasticity of intertemporal substitution), and to an additional carbon tax if the hazard rate is endogenous and depends on the stock of greenhouse gases. The total carbon tax splits into a conventional carbon tax that corrects for marginal damages of the stock of greenhouse gases, the additional carbon tax that corrects for the risk of climate tipping, and a third component that corrects for the effect of a high stock of greenhouse gases on the marginal damages after climate tipping. The second and the third component follow from the term $h(p)\left(V_b(k,p) - V_a(k,p)\right)$ in the Hamilton–Jacobi–Bellman equation before climate tipping that reflects the risk of tipping into a regime with the lower current value $V_a < V_b$. The terms

$h'(p)\Big(V_b(k,p) - V_a(k,p)\Big)$ and $h(p)\Big(V_{bp}(k,p) - V_{ap}(k,p)\Big)$ result from the differentiation with respect to the stock of greenhouse gases p. The first term is the higher risk of climate tipping by an increase in this stock. The second term splits into a term that shows up in the discount rate and a term that shows the decrease in the current value after climate tipping V_a by an increase in the stock of greenhouse gases p (Equation 80). This last term raises the stakes for the risk of climate tipping, which must also be corrected by the carbon tax.

The calibration shows that optimal saving is precautionary for reasonable values of the elasticity of intertemporal substitution, so that the Ramsey growth model targets for a higher steady-state capital stock than when climate tipping is ignored. The calibration also shows that the total carbon tax is much higher than when climate tipping is ignored. Furthermore, the components in the total carbon tax that correct for the risk of climate tipping and lower the stakes of climate tipping are much higher than the component that corrects for the marginal damages.

The literature on the risk of climate tipping is growing rapidly (Pindyck, 2013). Cai et al. (2012) and Lemoine and Traeger (2014) analyze the effect of possible climate tipping points in the DICE model. They also find a significant increase in the social cost of carbon. This Element focuses on the theory of climate tipping in the framework of the Ramsey growth model, with a calibration to illustrate the results. The policy conclusion is that ignoring potential climate tipping points is a big mistake when considering climate policy to curb greenhouse gas emissions.

5 Conclusion

Ecologists have observed and analyzed the occurrence of tipping points or regime shifts in many ecological systems. When valuable activities lead to pollution of ecosystems, which can then lead to tipping in ecosystems and cause a substantial loss of valuable ecosystem services, economics in the presence of tipping points is born. This Element starts with several examples of tipping points in ecosystems and the corresponding management options and issues. However, the main part of this Element focuses on two distinct approaches to this problem.

If a model of the ecosystem with tipping points exists, the problem becomes a cost–benefit analysis with the loss of ecosystem services as the cost and the polluting activities as the benefit. Tipping or a regime shift means a structural change in the ecosystem dynamics, which is hard or impossible to reverse and implies a substantial loss of ecosystem services. The lake is the classical example. Optimal management of the phosphorus loadings steers the lake to the oligotrophic regime with a high level of ecosystem services or to the eutrophic regime with a low level of ecosystem services. If the cost of losing ecosystem services is relatively high, it is optimal to end up in the oligotrophic regime. However, for a lower cost, it depends on the initial condition of the lake whether it is better to end up in the oligotrophic regime or in the eutrophic regime. The initial condition where optimal management is indifferent is called a Skiba point. When the lake is common property, increasing the number of users has a similar effect. If the cost is such that it is collectively optimal to end up in the oligotrophic regime, the open-loop Nash equilibrium of this differential game ends up in the eutrophic regime when the pollution of the lake is already too high. The feedback Nash or Markov perfect equilibrium of this differential game has the property that the lake gets out of the eutrophic regime, but welfare is lower than under optimal management. Tipping points or regime shifts have a positive message when considering partial cooperation. As expected, lowering the cost of losing ecosystem services requires a higher level of cooperation to prevent tipping to the eutrophic regime or to induce tipping back to the oligotrophic regime. In contrast with the usual grim story, however, such a coalition of users is stable up to a higher level than in the absence of a tipping point. Finally, these analyses use a one-dimensional reduced form of the lake model. However, a two-dimensional system with fast-slow dynamics is needed to describe the precise behavior of the lake. Optimal management of this full lake model has Skiba points in the sense of indifference between moving to the oligotrophic or to the eutrophic regime but also has Skiba points in the sense of indifference between two paths leading to the same long-run steady state in either the oligotrophic or eutrophic regime. Dynamical optimization with fast-slow dynamics requires advanced numerical methods. Extensions to other issues are still open and left for future research.

If a precise model of the ecosystem does not exist but tipping or a regime shift is expected to occur, the problem becomes a standard economic problem with an uncertain shock to a parameter due to tipping driven by a hazard rate. An example is a fishery where a shock to the carrying capacity can occur due to tipping in the ecological system to which the fish belongs. Another example is Ramsey growth, where a shock to the total factor productivity can occur due to climate tipping. In a fishery model with a fixed price, a constant hazard rate does not change the harvesting behavior, but an endogenous hazard rate that increases for a decreasing fish stock leads to precautionary behavior. In a fishery model with a *CRRA* utility of harvest, a constant hazard rate can lead to precaution or to increased exploitation, depending on the elasticity of inter-temporal substitution. In the Ramsey growth model, a constant hazard rate can lead in the same way to precautionary saving or to less saving. An endogenous hazard rate that increases for an increasing stock of greenhouse gases leads to a higher social cost of carbon, and thus requires an additional carbon tax. If the carbon tax also corrects for marginal damages to the total factor productivity, it has this conventional component, and a component that corrects for the risk of tipping, and one that corrects for decreasing the value of the problem after tipping because of increasing the stock of greenhouse gases. A calibration with real-world data and with reasonable parameter values shows that saving should be precautionary, and that the carbon tax should be much higher than in the absence of climate tipping. The additional components of the carbon tax are much higher than the conventional component.

Tipping or regime shifts occur in dynamical models. Economics optimizes net benefits, profits, or utility. This implies that the core methodology is dynamical optimization or optimal control. The analysis of the lake system employs optimal control with concave–convex constraints, and extends this to a differential game, which is optimal control with several users. The analyses of the fishery and Ramsey growth employ optimal control before and after tipping. Using dynamic programming for the optimal control problem before tipping is convenient because it turns the problem with an uncertain finite horizon into a deterministic problem with an infinite horizon.

Tipping points have become an important concept in the description of the behavior of ecological systems. Recent developments in the theory of environmental economics focus on tipping points or regime shifts. The purpose of this Element is to present these developments and show how to handle problems in environmental economics in the presence of tipping points (an earlier version appeared in de Zeeuw, 2014). The main part of this Element chooses to present a precise account of the analysis of three typical models, instead of presenting a general overview of the analysis of tipping points in environmental economics theory. The idea is that such a precise account may help in developing other applications of the concepts and techniques that are used when analyzing other problems in environmental economics in the presence of tipping points.

References

Acemoglu, D., Aghion, P., Bursztyn, L., & Hemous, D. (2012). The environment and directed technical change. *The American Economic Review*, **102**(1), 131–66.

Arrow, K. J., & Fisher, A. C. (1974). Environmental preservation, uncertainty, and irreversibility. *The Quarterly Journal of Economics*, **88**(2), 312–9.

d'Aspremont, C., Jacquemin, A., Gabszewicz, J. J., & Weymark, J. A. (1983). On the stability of collusive price leadership. *The Canadian Journal of Economics*, **16**(1), 17–25.

Bala, G., Caldeira, K., & Nemani, R. (2010). Fast versus slow response in climate change: Implications for the global hydrological cycle. *Climate Dynamics*, **35**(2–3), 423–34.

Barrett, S. (1994). Self-enforcing international environmental agreements. *Oxford Economic Papers*, **46**, 878–94.

Barrett, S. (2013). Climate treaties and approaching catastrophes. *Journal of Environmental Economics and Management*, **66**(2), 235–50.

Barrett, S., & Dannenberg, A. (2012). Climate negotiations under scientific uncertainty. *Proceedings of the National Academy of Sciences*, **109**(43), 17372–6.

Başar, T., & Olsder, G.-J. (1982). *Dynamic Noncooperative Game Theory*, New York: Academic Press.

Berkes, F., Hughes, T. P., Steneck, R. S., Wilson, J. A., Bellwood, D. R., Crona, B., Folke, C., Gunderson, L. H., Leslie, H. M., Norberg, J., Nyström, M., Olsson, P., Österblom, H., Scheffer, M., & Worm, B. (2006). Globalization, roving bandits, and marine resources. *Science*, **311**(5767), 1557–8.

Biggs, R., Blenckner, T., Folke, C., Gordon, L. J., Norström, A., Nyström, M., & Peterson, G. D. (2012). Regime shifts. In A. Hastings & L. Gross, eds., *Encyclopedia in Theoretical Ecology*, Berkeley and Los Angeles: University of California Press, pp. 609–16.

Bikhchandani, S., Hirshleifer, D., & Welch, I. (1992). A theory of fads, fashion, custom, and cultural change as informational cascades. *Journal of Political Economy*, **100**(5), 992–1026.

Brock, W. A., & Carpenter, S. R. (2006). Variance as a leading indicator of regime shift in ecosystem services. *Ecology and Society*, **11**(2), 9.

Brock, W. A., & Starrett, D. (2003). Managing systems with non-convex positive feedback. *Environmental and Resource Economics*, **26**(4), 575–602.

Cai, Y., Judd, K. L., & Lontzek, T. S. (2012). The social cost of abrupt climate change. *Working Paper*, Stanford, CA: Hoover Institution, Stanford University.

Carpenter, S. R. (2003). *Regime Shifts in Lake Ecosystems: Pattern and Variation*, Excellence in Ecology 15, Oldendorf/Luhe: International Ecology Institute.

Carpenter, S. R. (2005). Eutrophication of aquatic ecosystems: Bistability and soil phosphorus. *Proceedings of the National Academy of Sciences*, **102**(29), 10002–5.

Carpenter, S. R., Ludwig, D., & Brock, W. A. (1999). Management of eutrophication for lakes subject to potentially irreversible change. *Ecological Applications*, **9**(3), 751–71.

Carraro, C., & Siniscalco, D. (1993). Strategies for the international protection of the environment. *Journal of Public Economics*, **52**(3), 309–28.

Clark, C. W. (1990). *Mathematical Bioeconomics: The Optimal Management of Renewable Resources*, New York: John Wiley & Sons.

Clarke, H. R., & Reed, W. J. (1994). Consumption/pollution tradeoffs in an environment vulnerable to pollution-related catastrophic collapse. *Journal of Economic Dynamics and Control*, **18**(5), 991–1010.

Crépin, A.-S. (2007). Using fast and slow processes to manage resources with thresholds. *Environmental and Resource Economics*, **36**(2), 191–213.

Crépin, A.-S., Biggs, R., Polasky, S., Troell, M., & de Zeeuw, A. (2012). Regime shifts and management. *Ecological Economics*, **84**, 15–22.

Crépin, A.-S., Norberg, J., & Mäler, K. G. (2011). Coupled economic-ecological systems with slow and fast dynamics: Modelling and analysis method. *Ecological Economics*, **70**(8), 1448–58.

Cropper, M. L. (1976). Regulating activities with catastrophic environmental effects. *Journal of Environmental Economics and Management*, **3**(1), 1–15.

Crutzen, P. J. (2006). Albedo enhancement by stratospheric sulfur injections: A contribution to resolve a policy dilemma? *Climate Change*, **77**(3–4), 211–9.

Dasgupta, P. (1982). *The Control of Resources*, Cambridge, MA: Harvard University Press.

Dechert, W. D., & O'Donnell, S. I. (2006). The stochastic lake game: A numerical solution. *Journal of Economic Dynamics and Control*, **30**(9–10), 1569–87.

Diekert, F. K. (2017). Threatening thresholds? The effect of disastrous regime shifts on the non-cooperative use of environmental goods and services. *Journal of Public Economics*, **147**, 30–49.

Dockner, E. J., & Long, N. V. (1993). International pollution control: Cooperative versus noncooperative strategies. *Journal of Environmental Economics and Management*, **25**(1), 13–29.

Dockner, E., & Wagener, F. (2014). Markov perfect Nash equilibria in models with a single capital stock. *Economic Theory*, **56**(3), 585–625.

Duffie, D., & Epstein, L. G. (1992). Stochastic differential utility. *Econometrica*, **60**(2), 353–94.

Elmquist, T., Folke, C., Nyström, M., Peterson, G., Bengtsson J., Walker, B., & Norberg, J. (2003). Response diversity, ecosystem change and resilience. *Frontiers in Ecology and in the Environment*, **1**(9), 488–94.

Epstein, L. G., & Zin, S. E. (1989). Substitution, risk aversion, and the temporal behavior of consumption and asset returns: A theoretical framework. *Econometrica*, **57**(4), 937–69.

Folke, C., Carpenter, S., Walker, B., Scheffer, M., Elmquist, T., Gunderson, L., & Holling, C. S. (2004). Regime shifts, resilience, and biodiversity in ecosystem management. *Annual Review of Ecology, Evolution, and Systematics*, **35**, 557–81.

Gjerde, J., Grepperud, S., & Kverndokk, S. (1999). Optimal climate policy under the possibility of a catastrophe. *Resource and Energy Economics*, **21**(3–4), 289–317.

Gladwell, M. (2000). *The Tipping Point: How Little Things Can Make a Big Difference*, New York: Little, Brown & Company.

Gollier, C., & Treich, N. (2003). Decision-making under scientific uncertainty: The economics of the precautionary principle. *Journal of Risk and Uncertainty*, **27**(1), 77–103.

Golosov, M., Hassler, J., Krusell, P., & Tsyvinski, A. (2014). Optimal taxes on fossil fuel in general equilibrium. *Econometrica*, **82**(1), 41–88.

Grass, D., Kiseleva, T., & Wagener, F. (2015). Small-noise asymptotics of Hamilton–Jacobi–Bellman equations and bifurcations of stochastic optimal control problems. *Communications in Nonlinear Science and Numerical Simulation*, **22**(1–3), 38–54.

Grass, D., Xepapadeas, A., & de Zeeuw, A. (2017). Optimal management of ecosystem services with pollution traps: The lake model revisited. *Journal of the Association of Environmental and Resource Economists*, **4**(4), 1121–54.

Hamilton, L., Lyster, P., & Otterstad, O. (2000). Social change, ecology and climate in 20th-Century Greenland. *Climate Change*, **47**(1–2), 193–211.

Hardin, G. (1968). The tragedy of the commons. *Science*, **162**(3859), 1243–8.

Heijdra, B. J., & Heijnen, P. (2013). Environmental abatement and the macro-economy in the presence of ecological thresholds. *Environmental and Resource Economics*, **55**(1), 47–70.

Hein, L. (2006). Cost-efficient eutrophication control in a shallow lake ecosystem subject to two steady states. *Ecological Economics*, **59**(4), 429–39.

Hoel, M. (1992). International environmental conventions: The case of uniform reduction of emissions. *Environmental and Resource Economics*, **2**(2), 141–59.

Holling, C. S. (1959). The components of predation as revealed by a study of small-mammal predation of the European pine sawfly. *The Canadian Entomologist*, **91**(5), 293–320.

Hughes, T. P., Baird, A. H., Bellwood, D. R., Card, M., Connelly, S. R., Folke, C., Grosberg, R., Hoegh-Guldberg, O., Jackson, J. B. C., Kleypas, J., Lough, J. M., Marshall, P., Nyström, M., Palumbi, S. R., Pandolfi, J. M., Rosen, B., & Roughgarden, J. (2003). Climate change, human impacts, and the resilience of coral reefs. *Science*, **301**(5635), 929–33.

Jaakkola, N., & Wagener, F. (2023). Differential games of public investment: Markovian best responses in the general case. *CESifo Working Paper*, 10585.

Janssen, M. A., Anderies, J. M., & Walker, B. H. (2004). Robust strategies for managing rangelands with multiple stable attractors. *Journal of Environmental Economics and Management*, **47**(1), 140–62.

Janssen, M. A., & Carpenter, S. R. (1999). Managing the resilience of lakes: A multi-agent modeling approach. *Conservation Ecology*, **3**(2), 15.

Kamien, M. I., & Schwartz, N. L. (1971). Optimal maintenance and sale age for a machine subject to failure. *Management Science*, **17**(8), B495–504.

Keller, K., Bolker, B. M., & Bradford, D. F. (2004). Uncertain climate thresholds and optimal economic growth. *Journal of Environmental Economics and Management*, **48**(1), 723–41.

Kossioris, G., Plexousakis, M., Xepapadeas, A., & de Zeeuw, A. (2011). On the optimal taxation of common-pool resources. *Journal of Economic Dynamics and Control*, **35**(11), 1868–79.

Kossioris, G., Plexousakis, M., Xepapadeas, A., de Zeeuw, A., & Mäler, K.-G. (2008). Feedback Nash equilibria for non-linear differential games in pollution control. *Journal of Economic Dynamics and Control*, **32**(4), 1312–31.

Koutsimpela, A., & Loulakis, M. (2024). On the optimally controlled stochastic shallow lake. *International Journal of Control*, **97**(11), 2539–51.

Kreps, D. M., & Porteus, E. L. (1978). Temporal resolution of uncertainty and dynamic choice theory. *Econometrica*, **46**(1), 185–200.

Krugman, P. (1991). History versus expectations. *The Quarterly Journal of Economics*, **106**(2), 651–67.

Lemoine, D., & Traeger, C. (2014). Watch your step: Optimal policy in a tipping climate. *American Economic Journal: Economic Policy*, **6**(1), 137–66.

Lemoine, D., & Traeger, C. (2016). Ambiguous tipping points. *Journal of Economic Behavior and Organization*, **132**(B), 5–18.

Lenton, T. M., Held, H., Kriegler, E., Hall, J. W., Lucht, W., Rahmstorf, S., & Schellnhuber, H. J. (2008). Tipping elements in the Earth's climate system. *Proceedings of the National Academy of Sciences*, **105**(6), 1786–93.

Ludwig, D., Jones, D. D., & Holling, C. S. (1978). Qualitative analysis of insect outbreak systems: The spruce budworm and forest. *Journal of Animal Ecology*, **47**, 315–32.

Mäler, K.-G., Xepapadeas, A., & de Zeeuw, A. (2003). The economics of shallow lakes. *Environmental and Resource Economics*, **26**(4), 603–24.

Meadows, D. H, Meadows, D. L., Randers, J., & Behrens III, W. W. (1972). *The Limits to Growth: A Report for the Club of Rome's Project on the Predicament of Mankind*, New York: Universe Books.

Miller, S., & Nkuiya, B. (2016). Coalition formation in fisheries with potential regime shift. *Journal of Environmental Economics and Management*, **79**, 189–207.

Monderer, D., & Shapley, L. S. (1996). Potential games. *Games and Economic Behavior*, **14**(1), 124–43.

Murphy, G. M. (1960). *Ordinary Differential Equations and their Solutions*, Princeton, NJ: Van Nostrand.

Norberg, J., Swaney, D. P., Dushoff, J., Lin, J., Casagrandi, R., & Levin, S. A. (2001). Phenotypic diversity and ecosystem functioning in changing environments: A theoretical framework. *Proceedings of the National Academy of Sciences*, **98**(20), 11376–81.

Nordhaus, W. D. (2008). *A Question of Balance: Weighing the Options on Global Warming Policies*, New Haven, CT: Yale University Press.

Nordhaus, W. (2014). Estimates of the social cost of carbon: Concepts and results from the DICE-2013R model and alternative approaches. *Journal of the Association of Environmental and Resource Economists*, **1**(1/2), 273–312.

Nyström, M., Folke, C., & Moberg, F. (2000). Coral reef disturbance and resilience in a human-dominated environment. *Trends in Ecology & Evolution*, **15**(10), 413–7.

Pindyck, R. S. (2013). The climate policy dilemma. *Review of Environmental Economics and Policy*, **7**(2), 219–37.

van der Ploeg, F., & de Zeeuw, A. (2016). Non-cooperative and cooperative responses to climate catastrophes in the global economy: The North–South perspective. *Environmental and Resource Economics*, **65**(3), 519–40.

van der Ploeg, F., & de Zeeuw, A. (2018). Climate tipping and economic growth: Precautionary capital and the price of carbon. *Journal of the European Economic Association*, **16**(5), 1577–617.

van der Ploeg, F., & de Zeeuw, A. (2019). Pricing carbon and adjusting capital to fend off climate catastrophes. *Environmental and Resource Economics*, **72** (1), 29–50.

Polasky, S., de Zeeuw, A., & Wagener, F. (2011). Optimal management with potential regime shifts. *Journal of Environmental Economics and Management*, **62**(2), 229–40.

Reed, W. J. (1984). The effects of the risk of fire on the optimal rotation of a forest. *Journal of Environmental Economics and Management*, **11**(2), 180–90.

Reed, W. J. (1988). Optimal harvesting of a fishery subject to random catastrophic collapse. *Mathematical Medicine and Biology*, **5**(3), 215–35.

Ren, B., & Polasky, S. (2014). The optimal management of renewable resources under the risk of potential regime shift. *Journal of Economic Dynamics and Control*, **40**(6), 195–212.

Richardson, K., Steffen, W., Lucht, W., Bendtsen, J., Cornell, S. E., Donges, J. F., Drüke, M., Fetzer, I., Bala, G., von Bloh, W., Feulner, G., Fiedler, S., Gerten, D., Gleeson, T., Hofmann, M., Huiskamp, W., Kummu, M., Mohan, C., Nogués-Bravo, D., Petri, S., Porkka, M., Rahmstorf, S., Schaphoff, S., Thonicke, K., Tobian, A., Virkki, V., Wang-Erlandsson, L., Weber, L., & Rockström, J. (2023). Earth beyond six of nine planetary boundaries. *Science Advances*, **9**(37), eadh2458.

Rinaldi, S., & Scheffer, M. (2000). Geometric analysis of ecological models with slow and fast processes. *Ecosystems*, **3**(6), 507–21.

Rockström, J., Steffen, W., Noone, K., Persson, A., Stuart Chapin III, F., Lambin, E. F., Lenton, T. M., Scheffer, M., Folke, C., Schellnhuber, H. J., Nykvist, B., de Wit, C. A., Hughes, T., van der Leeuw, S., Rodhe, H., Sörlin, S., Snyder, P. K., Constanza, R., Svedin, U., Falkenmark, M., Karlberg, L., Corell, R. W., Fabry, V. J., Hansen, J., Walker, B., Liverman, D., Richardson, K., Crutzen, P., & Foley, J.A. (2009). A safe operating space for humanity. *Nature*, **461**(7263), 472–5.

Rubio, S. J., & Casino, B. (2002). A note on cooperative versus non-cooperative strategies in international pollution control. *Resource and Energy Economics*, **24**(3), 251–61.

Scharfstein, D. S., & Stein, J. C. (1990). Herd behavior and investment. *The American Economic Review*, **80**(3), 465–79.

Scheffer, M. (1998). *Ecology of Shallow Lakes*, London: Chapman & Hall.

Scheffer, M., Bascompte, J., Brock, W. A., Brovkin, V., Carpenter, S. R., Dakes, V., Held, H., van Nes, E. H., Rietkerk, M., & Sugihara, G. (2009). Early-warning signals for critical transitions. *Nature*, **461**(7260), 53–9.

Scheffer, M., Carpenter, S., Foley, J. A., Folke, C., & Walker, B. (2001). Catastrophic shifts in ecosystems. *Nature*, **413**(6856), 591–6.

Skiba, A. K. (1978). Optimal growth with a convex-concave production function. *Econometrica*, **46**(3), 527–39.

Steneck, R. S., Hughes, T. P., Cinner, J. E., Adger, W. N., Arnold, S. N., Berkes, F., Boudreau, S. A., Brown, K., Folke, C., Gunderson, L., Olsson, P., Scheffer, M., Stephenson, E., Walker, B., Wilson, J., & Worm, B. (2011). Creation of a gilded trap by the high economic value of the Maine lobster fishery. *Conservation Biology*, **25** (5), 904–12.

Stern, N. (2007). *The Economics of Climate Change: The Stern Review*, Cambridge: Cambridge University Press.

Tsur, Y., & Zemel, A. (1996). Accounting for global warming risks: Resource management under event uncertainty. *Journal of Economic Dynamics and Control*, **20**(6–7), 1289–305.

Tsur, Y., & Zemel, A. (1998). Pollution control in an uncertain environment. *Journal of Economic Dynamics and Control*, **22**(6), 967–75.

Tsutsui, S., & Mino, K. (1990). Nonlinear strategies in dynamic duopolistic competition with sticky prices. *Journal of Economic Theory*, **52**(1), 136–61.

Verhulst, P.-F. (1838). Notice sur la loi que la population suit dans son accroissement. *Correspondence Mathématique et Physique*, **10**, 113–21.

Wagener, F. O. O. (2003). Skiba points and heteroclinic bifurcations, with applications to the shallow lake system. *Journal of Economic Dynamics and Control*, **27**(9), 1533–61.

Wagener, F., & de Zeeuw, A. (2021). Stable partial cooperation in managing systems with tipping points. *Journal of Environmental Economics and Management*, **109**, 102499.

Walker, B., Pearson, L., Harris, M., Mäler, K.-G., Li, C.-Z., Biggs, R., & Baynes, T. (2010). Incorporating resilience in the assessment of inclusive wealth: An example from South East Australia. *Environmental and Resource Economics*, **45**(2), 183–202.

Zeeman, E. C. (1976). Catastrophe theory. *Scientific American*, **234**(4), 65–83.

de Zeeuw, A. (2014). Regime shifts in resource management. *Annual Review of Resource Economics*, **6**, 85–104.

de Zeeuw, A., & He, X. (2017). Managing a renewable resource facing the risk of a regime shift in the ecological system. *Resource and Energy Economics*, **48**(7), 42–54.

Acknowledgments

I am grateful to Anastasios Xepapadeas, Karl-Göran Mäler, Rick van der Ploeg, Stephen Polasky, Florian Wagener, George Kossioris, Michael Plexousakis, Anne-Sophie Crépin, Reinette Biggs, Max Troell, Dieter Grass, and Xiaoli He for working together on these issues, and to Florian Wagener for providing Figures 2, 3, 4, 5 and 6.

Cambridge Elements ☰

Environmental, Natural Resource and Sustainable Development Economics

Athens University of Economics and Business
(Greece) & University of Cambridge (UK)

Professor Dr. Phoebe Koundouri is a globally renowned economist and a pioneer in the development of innovative, human-centered, interdisciplinary mathematical systems that support the sustainable interaction between nature, society, and the economy. She holds an MPhil and PhD from the University of Cambridge. She has held academic positions at leading institutions, including the University of Cambridge, University College London (UCL), the London School of Economics (LSE), the University of Reading, and the Technical University of Denmark. She is currently Professor of Economics at the Athens University of Economics and Business and the University of Cambridge, and Founder and Director of the AE4RIA Research Centres. Ranked among the top 1% of scientists worldwide, Professor Koundouri has authored 20 books and more than 700 peer-reviewed scientific papers, served as editor for numerous academic journals, and led over 100 international research projects across 120 countries. She has delivered keynote speeches and high-level policy addresses across all continents and at major international fora. She serves as Chief Scientist for the UN Global Sustainable Development Report 2027, is former President of the European Association of Environmental and Resource Economists (EAERE), and is currently President of the World Council of Environmental and Resource Economists Associations. She is also Chair of the UN SDSN Global Climate Hub, Co-Chair of SDSN Europe, and an advisor to numerous multilateral organizations and governments. A Fellow of numerous prestigious global, European, and national academies, and a member of the Nobel Prize in Economics Committee, she has received many distinguished awards and honors. These include a European Research Council Synergy Grant, the Academy of Athens Award for Science, and the Republic of Cyprus Excellence Award.

About the Series

The *Cambridge Elements* series in Environmental, Natural Resources and Sustainable Development Economics is part of the wider *Cambridge Elements* program, which publishes concise, peer-reviewed works by leading experts. Each volume (20,000–30,000 words) bridges the gap between journal articles and full-length books, offering a clear introduction to a key research area alongside original analysis and forward-looking perspectives.

This series offers accessible, interdisciplinary resources that address today's most pressing environmental, natural resource, and sustainability challenges. Bridging economics, ecology, decision theory, and policy, each volume synthesizes cutting-edge research, theoretical and mathematical insights, and practical case studies.

Designed for academics, policymakers, and advanced students, the series explores key topics such as climate economics, biodiversity conservation, social cost-benefit analysis, sustainable development, decision theory and policy design for sustainable economic transformations – all presented in a rigorous yet approachable format.

With a global perspective and contributions from a diverse community of top scholars, the series equips readers with the knowledge, models, and tools needed to understand and help shape the transition toward a sustainable relationship between nature, the economy, and society – one of the defining challenges of the 21st century.

Theory and Methods for Environmental, Natural Resource and Sustainable Development Economics

- AI, Machine Learning
- Cost Benefit Analysis
- Decision Theory, Uncertainty, Ambiguity
- Discounting
- Economic Instrument and Policy Design
- Experimental and Behavior Approaches
- Financial Economics and Econometrics
- Game Theory and Agent-based modelling
- General Equilibrium Analysis and Impact Assessment Models
- Macroeconomic and Microeconomic Modelling
- Non-Linearities and Tipping Points
- Open Science, Open Data, Digitalization
- Sustainable Business Modelling and ESG Strategies
- Sustainable Development: Modelling, Measurement, Pathways
- Time Series, Spatial, Panel Econometrics
- Valuation Methods

Thematic Areas for Environmental, Natural Resources and Sustainable Development Economics and Econometrics

- Biodiversity
- Circular Economy
- Energy
- Land Use and Land Use Change
- Marine Use
- Natural Resources Management
- Transport
- Water

Cambridge Elements ☰

Environmental, Natural Resource and Sustainable Development Economics

Elements in the Series

Environmental Economics in the Presence of Tipping Points
Aart de Zeeuw

A full series listing is available at: www.cambridge.org/EERE

For EU product safety concerns, contact us at Calle de José Abascal, 56–1°,
28003 Madrid, Spain or eugpsr@cambridge.org.

www.ingramcontent.com/pod-product-compliance
Ingram Content Group UK Ltd.
Pitfield, Milton Keynes, MK11 3LW, UK
UKHW022032310526

471684UK00010B/294